10-Minuten-Training ENGLISCH

Bleiben Sie fit - mit schnellen Übungen
für unterwegs und zwischendurch

von Kit Batten

Ernst Klett Sprachen GmbH
Barcelona • Belgrad • Budapest • Ljubljana • London • Posen • Prag
Sofia • Stuttgart • Zagreb

PONS
10-Minuten-Training
ENGLISCH

Bleiben Sie fit - mit schnellen Übungen
für unterwegs und zwischendurch

von Kit Batten

Dieses Werk ist inhaltlich identisch mit: „PONS QuickCheck Englisch“,
ISBN: 3-12-560588-1.

Dieses Werk folgt der amtlichen Regelung der deutschen
Rechtschreibung in der Fassung von 2006.

Auflage A1 6 5 4 3 / 2010 2009 2008 2007

Internet: www.pons.de
E-Mail: info@pons.de

Redaktion: Edda Vorrath-Wiesenthal, Elizabeth Webster
Zeichnungen: Ulrike Müller-Zimmermann, Heidelberg
Logoentwurf: Erwin Poell, Heidelberg
Logoüberarbeitung: Sabine Redlin, Ludwigsburg
Einbandgestaltung: Schmidt & Dupont
Titelfoto: Vlado Golub, Stuttgart
Satz: Satz und mehr, Besigheim
Druck: Legoprint
Printed in Italy.
ISBN: 978-3-12-561293-8

Zu diesem Buch

Sie beherrschen die englische Sprache schon recht gut. Halten Sie sich fit.

Mit **PONS 10-Minuten-Training** können Sie auf schnelle und unterhaltsame Weise Ihre Kenntnisse in Englisch überprüfen, erweitern und verbessern.

Sie können ganz flexibel – nach Lust und Laune – lernen: Es spielt keine Rolle, in welcher Reihenfolge Sie die Übungen bearbeiten.

Versuchen Sie zunächst, die Übungen ohne Zuhilfenahme der *Lösungen* zu bearbeiten. Danach können Sie Ihre Ergebnisse mit den Lösungen im hinteren Teil des Buches vergleichen. Dort finden Sie häufig auch Erklärungen dazu, weshalb eine Lösung richtig oder falsch ist.

Die **Tipps** bieten Ihnen darüber hinaus weitere nützliche Informationen zum Thema, zusätzlichen Wortschatz oder auch nützliche Hinweise zum Sprachenlernen.

Querverweise helfen Ihnen, weitere Informationen zu ähnlichen Themen an anderen Stellen im Buch zu finden.

Wörter und Begriffe, die Ihnen vielleicht unbekannt sind und die nicht im Lösungsteil übersetzt werden, können Sie im *Glossar* am Ende des Buches nachschlagen.

Beim Sprachenlernen wünschen wir Ihnen viel Spaß und Erfolg!

Inhalt

1

In the pub

A

Waren Sie schon einmal in einem typisch britischen Pub? Dann finden Sie sicher die acht Fehler, die in dem folgenden Text versteckt sind. Unterstreichen Sie, was falsch ist.

Last week I went into my local pub. It is just around the corner from where I live. It is called the White Hart and has a sign outside with a bunch of flowers arranged in a heart shape.

The landlord is a good friend of mine and over the years has earned a large amount of money from me. I sat at my usual table and he came over to me to ask what I wanted to drink. I asked for a half litre of beer as it was a very warm day and Fred, that is his name, brought it to me.

As it was not very busy I went to a shelf where the daily paper is kept and selected the local town evening newspaper. There was not very much new in it and I had soon read it.

After I had finished my first drink two friends came into the pub so I ordered a bottle of white wine for the three of us and we began to play bridge. Two hours later I was quite merry and had lost some money so I asked for the bill, paid and walked home.

B

Und kennen Sie sich aus, wenn es um die Bestellung geht? Finden Sie die richtige Übersetzung für die folgenden Ausdrücke.

1. [f] bitter
2. [a] shandy
3. [e] cider
4. [d] real ale
5. [h] ploughman's
6. [c] on tap
7. [b] white wine and soda
8. [g] pork scratchings

a. Alsterwasser, Radler
b. Spritzer, Schorle
c. vom Fass
d. traditionell gebrautes Bier, mit der Hand gezapft
e. Apfelwein
f. klassisches britisches Bier mit der Farbe von Altbier
g. gesalzene Grieben
h. Brot mit Cheddarkäse und Garnierung

2

Holidays

In diesem Buchstabenraster sind (senkrecht und waagerecht) zehn Wörter für Dinge versteckt, die eine Familie mit in den Urlaub nimmt. Suchen Sie die Wörter, und schreiben Sie sie neben die jeweils richtige Definition.

T	O	Y	S	F	S	D	V
O	F	G	S	H	O	E	S
W	S	C	U	S	A	Z	W
E	S	N	N	F	P	J	I
L	U	K	G	C	M	C	M
A	I	L	L	V	N	A	S
X	T	B	A	L	L	M	U
H	C	K	S	N	M	E	I
P	A	S	S	P	O	R	T
L	S	H	E	S	W	A	D
O	E	B	S	D	T	F	C

1. Something to lie on or to dry yourself after a swim. towel = Handtuch

2. A general word for things to play with, especially for children. ball toys

3. Something to carry your clothes in when going on holiday. suitcase........................

4. Something to wear if it is a bright day.
sunglasses........................

5. Something to kick on the beach.
ball........................

6. Something to use so that you have some souvenirs to look at. camera........................

7. Something you need if you go abroad.
passport........................

8. Something to wear in the water.
swimsuit........................

9. Something you use to wash with.
soap........................

10. Something to wear on your feet.
shoes........................

3 Since = seit Zeitpkt.
for = Zeitraum

"Since" or "for"?

Für das deutsche Wort „seit" gibt es im Englischen die Wörter „since" und „for". Welches der beiden ist in den folgenden Sätzen jeweils richtig? Unterstreichen Sie.

1. I was born in Torquay and moved to Stuttgart after my studies. I have been living in Germany since/for 15 years.
2. I started teaching German students English after learning to speak German and I have been teaching adults since/for 13 years now. I really enjoy it.
3. I began teaching at a school but have been teaching freelance since/for 1985.
4. In 1972 I met a young girl from Stuttgart and we have been married since/for 19 years.
5. Most of our friends are German including Birgit and Uwe; we have known them since/for our daughters started at the same kindergarten.
6. My wife has been playing skittles with Birgit since/for January 1992. = Kegeln

7. I have been playing tennis regularly with Uwe since/for August last year.

8. Our daughters started school together and have been in the same class since/for six years.

9. They are both film fanatics and have been going to the cinema together since/for many years.

10. My wife saw a film with Kevin Costner and has been a fan of his since/for then.

4

O richtig

Correct response (1)

Nicht alle vier Antworten auf die folgenden Fragen sind richtig. Kreuzen Sie die möglichen Antworten an.

1. Can I take your coat for you?
- ☒ a) That's very kind of you.
- ☒ b) No.
- ☐ c) Yes it's very cold in here.
- ☒ d) I'd love it.

2. How do you do?
- ☒ a) Fine thanks.
- ☐ b) Pleased to meet you.
- ☒ c) Very well, thank you.
- ☐ d) How do you do?

3. Would you like a cup of tea?
- ☒ a) No thanks, I've just had one.
- ☒ b) I'd love one.
- ☒ c) No.
- ☐ d) I had one yesterday.

4. Shall I open the door for you?
- ☒ a) Yes. It's locked.
- ☐ b) It's broken.
- ☒ c) Yes please. That would help.
- ☒ d) I'll open it myself if you don't mind.

5. Would you mind opening the window?
- ☒ a) Yes. That's alright.
- ☒ b) No, not at all.
- ☒ c) Can't you do it yourself?
- ☒ d) That's very good of you.

I don't mind = es macht mir nichts aus.

6. May I smoke?

☒ a) Smoking is not allowed in here.
☒ b) No.
☐ c) Smoking is bad for your health.
☐ d) Yes, that's alright. I don't mind.

7. Could I borrow your dictionary for a moment?

☐ a) Yes, certainly.
☒ b) No, I'm afraid not. I need it.
☒ c) No, certainly not!
☒ d) Only if you return it immediately.

8. You're married, aren't you?

☒ a) No, I'm not.
☐ b) I have two children.
☒ c) Yes, fifteen years.
☐ d) I'm a single person.

present perfect! immer noch aktuell

9. How long have you lived here?

☒ a) I lived here six years.
☒ b) We've lived here for fourteen years.
☐ c) We've stayed in this house two years now.
☐ d) Since Christmas.

10. What do you do?

☒ a) I'm a teacher.
☒ b) I'm learning some English for the test tomorrow.
☒ c) I'm playing my guitar.
☒ d) I am responsible for the computer network in our company.

11. Thank you very much for doing that.

☐ a) Please.
☐ b) Thank you.
☒ c) You're welcome.
☐ d) No, thank you.

5

“Do” or “make”?

Do oder make? Unterstreichen Sie das richtige Wort.

1. It is difficult homework but do/make your best to finish it.
2. Waiter, this meat is off. I’d like to do/make a complaint.
3. I have a lot of work to do/make before I can go home.
4. Could you do/make me a favour and lend me five pounds until tomorrow?
5. The coffee machine is broken. We will have to do/make without coffee during the break.
6. Oh no! I have done/made a mistake and printed it upside down!
7. This work is not good enough. You have to do/make it again.
8. Can I pay by cheque? And who do I do/make the cheque out to?
9. Would you like a coffee? I am just doing/making some.

10. We used to have a clocking-in machine but we did/made away with it three years ago.

11. Sally is very good with her hands, she did/made a beautiful puppet out of clay.

12. I have too much work. I could do/make with some help.

6

Food and drink

Die Buchstaben der folgenden Wörter für verschiedene Lebensmittel sind ein wenig durcheinandergeraten. Können Sie aus den Buchstaben die richtigen Wörter bilden? Als Hilfe finden Sie jeweils darunter eine kurze Definition.

1. RATSCOR ....
   reddish-orange vegetables

2. CUBECRUMS ....
   long and green salad ingredients

3. PINCASH ....
   green leaf ... not popular with everyone

4. HESCOOLCAT ....
   sweet and usually brown

5. RPAGES ....
   small fruits loved by wine growers

6. OTOASTME ....
   red salad fruit

7. SAUGASES ....
   traditional British breakfast ingredients

8. SIBISCUT ....
   eaten with a cup of tea or coffee

9. WIREBARS REST ....
red fruit, they are a hit at Wimbledon

10. IEJUNECARGO ....
a drink for breakfast (two words)

11. NOISNO ....
they will make you cry

12. PUREFIGART ....
a citrus breakfast

13. TAPESIGHT ....
an Italian speciality

14. WISHDANCES ....
for taking on a picnic

15. MICERACE ....
cool (two words)

7

Abbreviations

Kennen Sie die folgenden Abkürzungen? Schreiben Sie auf, wofür die einzelnen Buchstaben stehen oder was Sie damit verbinden.

1. BBC ....
2. AA ....
3. RSVP ....
4. BC and AD ....
5. CIA ....
6. c/o ....
7. DIY ....
8. FBI ....
9. GCSE ....
10. GMT ....
11. IOU ....

12. MCP ....

13. MOT ....

14. OAP ....

15. PR ....

16. PTO ....

17. SOS ....

18. UFO ....

19. VAT ....

20. VIP ....

21. etc. ....

22. e.g. ....

23. i.e. ....

24. B.A. ....

25. Ph.D. ....

8

Prefix

Durch das Voranstellen einer Vorsilbe lassen sich die fett gedruckten Wörter in ihr Gegenteil verwandeln. Aber aufgepasst: Es muss die richtige Vorsilbe gefunden werden.

un ● ir ● im ● dis ● in

1. She wore **clean** clothes. ....
2. He was a **grateful** man. ....
3. **Fortunately** we found it. ....
4. A **furnished** house. ....
5. It was a **human** reaction. ....
6. The **employed** man. ....
7. He **appeared** suddenly. ....
8. The dog was **hurt.** ....
9. A **comfortable chair.** ....
10. A **possible** solution. ....

11. A **fair** game. ....

12. The **fit** sportsman. ....

13. A **common** problem. ....

14. I **like** loud music. ....

15. An **expensive car.** ....

16. A **responsible** worker. ....

17. He was **conscious** after the fall. ....

18. We were in **agreement.** ....

19. A **formal** meeting. ....

20. He is **dependent** on his father. ....

9

Greeting cards

Was sagt oder schreibt man zu besonderen Anlässen als Glückwunsch? Ordnen Sie die Karten den Anlässen zu.

1. ☐ 2. ☐ 3. ☐

4. ☐ 5. ☐ 6. ☐

7. ☐ 8. ☐

9. ☐ 10. ☐

a) On someone's 40th birthday
b) On someone's 50th birthday
c) On the birth of a child
d) On getting married
e) At Christmas
f) On someone's 13th birthday
g) On any birthday
h) On passing the driving test
i) After 50 years of marriage
j) On someone's 18th birthday

10

Then and now

„Used to“ oder „to be used to“: Welche Form passt? Setzen Sie in den folgenden Sätzen die jeweils richtige ein. Nicht vergessen: Nach „(not) to be used to“ steht das Verb in der -ing-Form, nach „used to“ steht der Infinitiv (Grundform).

1. When we lived in Hamburg we .... (play) tennis regularly, but it is too expensive here.

2. Because of his job as a postman Arthur .... (get up) early in the morning.

3. Tina is a hair stylist. She .... (cut) her friends' hair for them.

4. When David was young he .... (play) handball for the local team.

5. My father has broken his right arm and cannot write letters as he .... (write) with his left hand.

6. When soldiers attacked a castle, the people in the castle .... (throw) rubbish and hot oil on their heads.

7. When Lenin was a young man he did not .... (believe) it was right for 5% of the people to have 95% of a country's wealth.

8. Between 1984 and 1989 Franziska .... (swim) five hours every day.

9. Sam did not .... (think) a computer would be useful until he bought one cheap at a sale.

10. Although Bob bought himself an electronic translator he still .... (use) it.

11

The human body

Benennen Sie die verschiedenen Körperteile.

1 ....
2 ....
3 ....
4 ....
5 ....
6 ....
7 ....
8 ....
9 ....
10 ....
11 ....
12 ....
13 ....
14 ....
15 ....
16 ....
17 ....
18 ....
19 ....
20 ....

1
2
3
4
5
6
7
8
9
10
11
12
13
14
15
16
17
18
19
20

12

Adjective or adverb?

Die drei kleinen Geschichten sind gespickt mit Adjektiven und Adverbien. Aber welche Form ist jeweils die richtige? Unterstreichen Sie sie.

1. David drives a red Pontiac Firebird. Although it looks fast my friend drives quite careful/carefully. Last week he had an accident. He was driving slow/slowly when a dog ran in front of his car. Thanks to his quick/quickly reactions he managed to stop the car very quick/quickly and the dog was not serious/seriously hurt.

2. Sheila is a student at University. She always does her work very careful/carefully. In her spare time she likes jazz dance and is an excellent/excellently

dancer. She likes travelling and she can speak four languages fluent/fluently. As she only has a small kitchen she is not very interested in cooking and is not a good/well cook. However, last Wednesday she cooked a chicken curry that tasted really good/well.

3. George and Judith live in an expensive/expensively house in Manchester. Last month they were pleased because they bought some pieces of furniture quite cheap/cheaply. They asked to have the items delivered to their house as quick/quickly as possible. The driver and his assistant unloaded the lorry and carried the heavy/heavily things into the house. As they were carrying an antique desk it fell heavy/heavily onto the floor. The drawers fell out and were bad/badly damaged. The transport company paid for the damage.

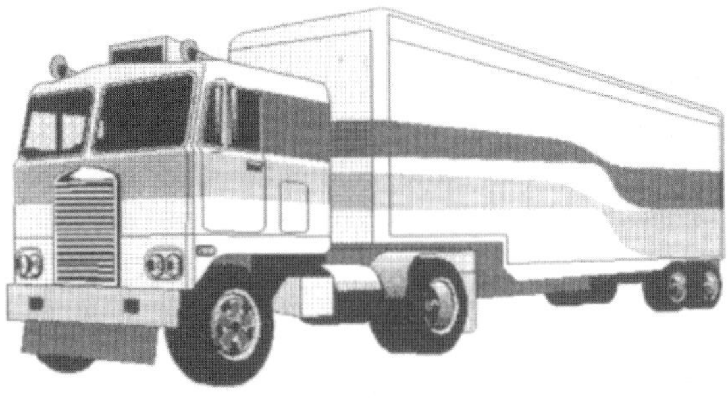

13

Childhood memories

Lesen Sie den folgenden Text. Im Anschluss sind die Definitionen von sieben Wörtern angegeben, die alle im Text zu finden sind. Um welche Wörter handelt es sich? Schreiben Sie sie jeweils neben die Definition.

THE HIGHLAND ROAD MOB

When I was a kid, between the ages of eight and fourteen, I was a member of a gang. We did not have a special name for our group; we were the Highland Road Mob because we all lived in Highland Road. There were about eight of us including my sister, Tina, who was a real tomboy; she played rough games just like the boys did.

We had an initiation ceremony. If a new person wanted to join our group or if we wanted to have a new recruit we would make the newcomer do something difficult as a test. Perhaps they would have to steal something from home for us to eat or perhaps they would have to do something dangerous like stealing apples from the local farmer's orchard. They also needed a sponsor, someone who would vouch for them and say they were OK.

As our street was the last one before the end of town we often played in the fields behind our homes. This was our turf and we visited the farms and orchards a kilometre away. In the autumn we stole apples, this is called scrumping in our dialect, or we collected conkers from the horse chestnut trees. We would put the conkers on a string and play a game with them. We played "hide-and-seek" in the woods or played "Cowboys and Indians." We thought we were the greatest. We were savvy – we knew what was happening! We had fun!

1. A group of people who do things together:

   ....

2. A girl who plays as if she were a boy:

   ....

3. A style of playing where you fight and do wild things: ....

4. A place where fruit trees can be found:

   ....

5. The area that a gang rules:

   ....

6. A dialect word for stealing apples:

   ....

7. The fruit of the horse chestnut used in some games: ....

14

Phrasal verbs

Viele Verben erhalten durch eine Präposition eine andere Bedeutung. Wählen Sie die richtige Präposition aus und setzen Sie sie ein.

1. Last week Bob took me .... We went to the cinema.

   out ● in ● off ● up

2. Recently I have taken .... fishing. It is an extremely relaxing hobby.

   out ● in ● off ● up

3. It was so hot yesterday that as soon as I got home I took .... all my clothes and slipped on my bikini.

   out ● in ● off ● up

4. He was really upset when his goldfish died. It took him six weeks to get .... it.

   over ● by ● out of ● up

5. My son started college last week and moved into his new flat. I do not know if he will get .... as usually we have to do everything for him.

   over ● by ● out of ● up

6. I like my new job but I hate getting .... so early in the morning.

   over ● by ● out ● up

7. Before I bought my new car I hired one for the weekend to try it ....

   on ● by ● out ● up

8. My colleague is always trying it .... at work. He comes late, leaves early and asks for overtime!

   on ● by ● out ● for

9. I am not happy with my present job. I am going to try .... a new one as soon as possible.

   on ● by ● out ● for

10. Tom never does his homework but he never runs .... excuses as to why he was not able to.

    after ● by ● out of ● into

11. On Saturday I ran .... an old schoolfriend of mine in the local supermarket.

    over ● up ● out ● into

12. Sheila is terrible. She is always running .... the boss. She really wants to go out with him.

    after ● by ● out of ● into

15

Did you know? (1)

Richtig oder falsch? Wie gut kennen Sie sich in der englischsprachigen Welt aus? Kreuzen Sie die richtige Antwort an.

1. George Washington was president of the United States. There is a story that as a boy he cut down a cherry tree. When his father asked him if he had done it, Washington said:
   - ☐ a) "I cannot tell a lie."
   - ☐ b) "It was not me."
   - ☐ c) "It was my brother."

2. John Brown, the hero of the song, was a real person who lived in the 19th Century and was killed because of his beliefs. Why was he executed?
   - ☐ a) For religious beliefs.
   - ☐ b) For murder.
   - ☐ c) For supporting the blacks' fight against slavery.

3. Father Christmas or Santa Claus is believed to live at the North Pole and has little helpers to make and parcel the presents for the children. He has a reindeer with a red nose. What is the reindeer's name?
   - ☐ a) Rudolph.
   - ☐ b) Randolph.
   - ☐ c) Fred.

4. Sir Walter Raleigh was a famous sailor at the time of Queen Elizabeth I. He is said to have brought the potato and tobacco to Europe. He had his head cut off in the Tower of London. Why was he executed?
   - ☐ a) For bringing lung cancer to Europe.
   - ☐ b) Because of the Irish potato famine.
   - ☐ c) For a failed expedition.

5. Florence Nightingale was born into a good family but wanted to do something useful so she followed the army to war. She worked a lot in army hospitals and introduced ideas that we expect from nurses today. She developed these ideas during:
   - ☐ a) the First World War.
   - ☐ b) the Crimean War.
   - ☐ c) the Boer War in South Africa.

6. Abraham Lincoln was President of the United States and helped to abolish the slave trade. Where was he when he was killed?
   - ☐ a) At home.
   - ☐ b) At the cinema.
   - ☐ c) At the theatre.

7. Peanuts is a comic strip in America which was written by George Schultz. There are many characters including Charlie Brown and his dog. What is the dog's name?
   - ☐ a) Peanuts.
   - ☐ b) Tin-Tin.
   - ☐ c) Snoopy.

8. In many Chinese restaurants in America it is normal that at the end of the meal you get a biscuit. These are called fortune cookies. When you open the biscuit there is something inside, what is it?
   - ☐ a) Meat.
   - ☐ b) A message.
   - ☐ c) A small present.

16

At the cinema

Ergänzen Sie in jeder Lücke die richtige Präposition. Welches Wort erhalten Sie, wenn Sie außerdem im Kästchen rechts neben jedem Satz den in Klammern stehenden Buchstaben einsetzen?

at (A) ● in (B) ● on (C) ● by (D) ● next to (R)

1. Hello David. How are you? Which firm are you working .... now? ☐

2. Oh, hello Barbara. I'm fine. I'm working for Dodds & Co. .... the accounts department. ☐

3. Where are they? Is that the company right .... the church in High Street? ☐

4. Yes that's right. I joined them .... the end of January. ☐

5. Would you like to go to the cinema .... Friday? ☐

6. There's a good film on .... the Roxy called "The Magician and the Model". It starts at 8 o'clock. ☐

7. Yes, that would be great. How shall we get there? Do you want me to drive or shall we go .... bus? ☐

8. You can pick me up .... 7.30. ☐

9. Good, we can go .... my new car. ☐

10. Can you see it? It's parked over there .... the Mercedes. ☐

11. Impressive. I can see you are good .... choosing sports cars. See you on Friday. ☐

17

"Beech" or "beach"?

Es gibt englische Wörter, die zwar gleich ausgesprochen werden, jedoch eine andere Schreibweise und eine andere Bedeutung haben. Unterstreichen Sie in den Sätzen das passende Wort.

1. Yesterday we spent the day on the beech/beach.
2. We keep our wine down in our seller/cellar.
3. I have heard/herd that Harald won a beauty competition.
4. The wind blue/blew so hard that some of the slates on the roof fell off.
5. This exercise is not very good, I'm bored/board.
6. We sailed out past the orange boy/buoy and then set sail for France.
7. Robert did not look after his bike and one day he had an accident because the front break/brake failed.
8. My dog is very intelligent. When I say "Hear!"/"Here!" she comes.
9. The recent World Cup was a very fair/fare one.
10. When we were on holiday in Spain we went to a car higher/hire firm and got a jeep.

11. Barbara's mother was so upset she nearly pulled all her hare/hair out.

12. The animal park was lovely. They had foxes, wild pigs and they even had a white heart/hart.

13. Mike was so greedy he ate the whole/hole cake himself.

14. The key/quay did not fit so we had to get a worker to help us open the door.

15. My brother is going on a rail holiday but we will meat/meet in Madrid in two weeks.

16. Only a gipsy lady with a crystal ball knows/nose what the future will bring.

17. We took our picnic to the open-air pool and had sandwiches, apples and pears/pairs.

18. Tolstoy is famous for his book "War and Piece"/ "Peace".

19. There were rose/rows and rose/rows of people at the open-air concert.

20. The shopkeeper was very happy with his latest sale, he had made 100% prophet/profit.

18

Celebrations

Die folgenden Aussagen betreffen Feiertage in den USA bzw. in Großbritannien. Aber Vorsicht: Manche Aussagen sind falsch. Kennzeichnen Sie mit R *für richtig oder* F *für falsch.*

1. ☐ The Americans celebrate Guy Fawkes Night on November 5th every year.
2. ☐ The British open their Christmas presents on December 24th.
3. ☐ The fourth of June is a public holiday in America.
4. ☐ American children celebrate Halloween more than British children.
5. ☐ Americans call their November holiday Thanksgiving in memory of the first successful harvest of the second group of settlers in 1621.
6. ☐ If Christmas Day or New Year's Day falls on a Saturday or Sunday then the bank holiday is lost in Britain.
7. ☐ In Britain and America New Year's Eve is known as Silvester.
8. ☐ In Britain the Queen has two birthdays.

9. ☐ The day after Christmas Day is called Boxing Day in Britain and is a national holiday.

10. ☐ January 6th is not a holiday in Britain or America.

11. ☐ The British have two bank holidays, Spring Bank Holiday and August Bank Holiday, which always fall on a Monday.

12. ☐ Whitsun is celebrated on the seventh Sunday after Easter and the following day, Whit Monday, is usually a holiday in England, Wales and Ireland.

13. ☐ St. David is the patron saint of Scotland.

14. ☐ St. Patrick's Day is a big day in the USA.

15. ☐ Burns Night is celebrated on 25th January.

19

Who am I?

Hier werden vier berühmte Persönlichkeiten beschrieben. Schreiben Sie die Namen waagerecht in das Gitter. Die Initialen ergeben den Namen einer bekannten Popgruppe (5.).

1. I am an American female singer. I am over fifty but people say that I look much younger. I have made so many hit records I cannot remember them all. I was once married to a man named Ike and I made my first records with him. One of my biggest hits was "Private Dancer".

2. I was a famous film director. I was born in Britain but most of my films were made in America. The majority of them were thrillers, and they are regarded as classics in this field. One of my films was called "The Birds" and another was about a famous motel in America.

3. I was King of Southern England a long time ago. My friends were Lancelot, Merlin and the Knights of the Round Table. My sword was the famous Excalibur.

4. I am a very famous English female actor. I was the star in many great films. My love life is always in the newspapers. I have been married more often than Henry VIII of England and certainly more than Cleopatra. I played her in a film in which one of my husbands also had a small part.

5. We are a famous English pop group of the nineties. We have had a number of hits. We are five boys from Manchester and we put on a good stage show with super dance routines. Most of our fans are teenage girls. Three of our top ten hits were "Pray," "Relight my Fire" and "Babe," and we won an MTV award in 1994 for best group.

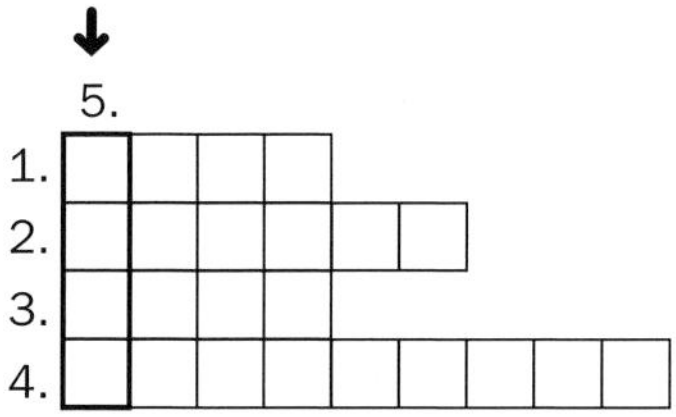

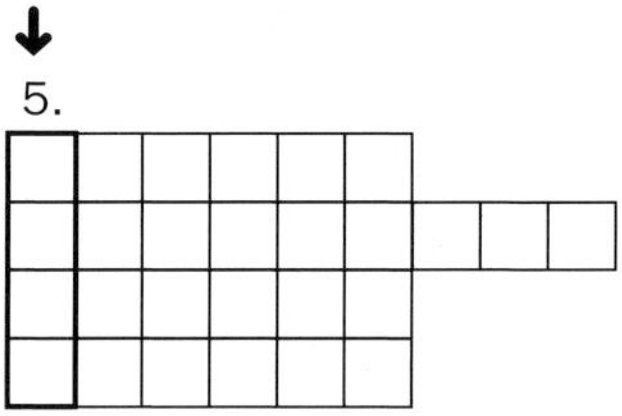

20

Complete the sentence

Ergänzen sie die folgenden Fragen mit dem passenden Wort und setzen Sie die Wörter in das Gitter ein. Welches Lösungswort ergibt sich?

1. I'm sorry, I didn't quite hear that. Can you .... it please?
2. Hello! How are ....?
3. Excuse me. Can you .... me the time please?
4. I'm new here. Could you give me some .... about the town?
5. We could meet next week. How .... Thursday?
6. How long have you been .... English?
7. Excuse me. Is your .... Thomas?

8. Have you got any .... brochures on Wales?

9. Good morning. Could I .... a table for two for tomorrow evening?

10. Did you say "Hughes"? Could you .... that for me?

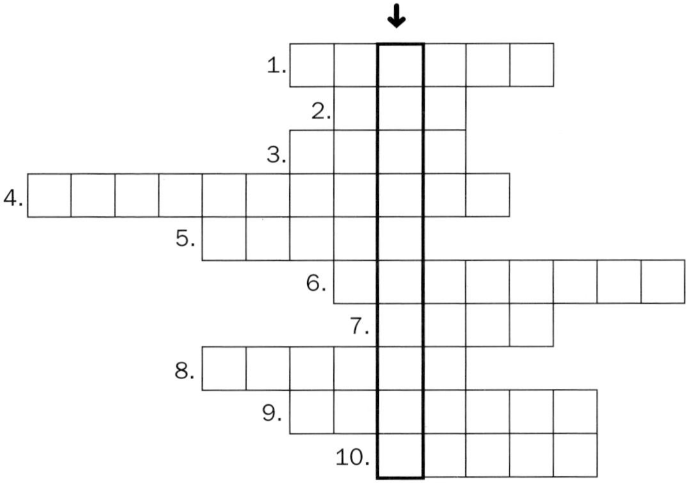

21

False friends (1)

Suchen Sie für die fett gedruckten Wörter eine geeignete Übersetzung.

1. Sally **engagiert sich** sehr für Umweltprobleme.

   ....

2. Ich habe soeben EUR 25,- **gespendet.**

   ....

3. Er hat eine **Karte** für das „Stones"-Konzert.

   ....

4. Kannst Du unserem Besuch Kaffee **kochen?**

   ....

5. Kannst Du meinen Fragebogen **kontrollieren**?

   ....

6. Seine große Leidenschaft sind **Oldtimer**.

   ....

7. Kann ich etwas Geld **ausleihen**?

   ....

8. Der Film war toll. Was **meinst** Du?

   ....

9. Morgen **muss** ich **nicht** nach Tokio.

   ....

10. Das Kind **will ein Eis.**

    ....

22

One word – two meanings

Die hier gesuchten Wörter haben mehr als eine Bedeutung. Finden Sie die Wörter, auf die beide Definitionen zutreffen.

1. not left / correct } ....
2. something to read / to reserve } ....
3. not warm / a slight illness } ....
4. symbol made up of two lines / to go over the road } ....
5. a small amount of liquid / to let fall } ....
6. to show (one's feelings) / super fast } ....
7. the front part of the head / to look at something } ....
8. blonde / gentlemanly at sport } ....
9. everything is OK / punishment for speeding or parking } ....
10. to sack / very hot situation } ....
11. large building of flats / to close a road } ....

12. nice and friendly
a sort of something } ....

13. the loser in the race
how long an event takes place } ....

14. to raise
to take somebody in your car } ....

15. to make different
coins } ....

16. presented in the theatre
to take part in game or sport } ....

17. to put a finger on a button
the papers } ....

18. a written account
to make a copy of sound } ....

19. not first
unit of time } ....

20. a group of words
to send to prison } ....

21. open space for a market
geometric shape } ....

22. small piece of paper
to fall, on ice for example } ....

23. needed to post a letter
put in one's passport } ....

24. three feet
open space or back garden } ....

23

"If" or "when"?

Kreuzen Sie in den folgenden Sätzen, die Sie in einem Restaurant hören könnten, „if" oder „when" an. Manchmal sind beide möglich.

1. ☐ If / ☐ When } the waiter comes I will order the fish.

2. ☐ If / ☐ When } they have fish then I will order it.

3. ☐ If / ☐ When } I have finished my wine I will order coffee for all of us.

4. ☐ If / ☐ When } I finish the main course, I certainly will not have room for any dessert!

5. ☐ If / ☐ When } the tiramisu is home-made I will definitely try some.

6. ☐ If / ☐ When } the bill comes I will pay it; it is my treat.

7. ☐ If / ☐ When } we leave you will have to drive.

8. ☐ If / ☐ When } I do not feel too full I will have a small ice cream.

9. ☐ If / ☐ When } there is a German white wine on the wine list, I will order a bottle.

10. ☐ If / ☐ When } the meal is not too expensive, I will recommend this restaurant to my friends.

11. ☐ If / ☐ When } the meal comes I will complain about the service.

12. ☐ If / ☐ When } the tomato soup comes, I will ask for Worcester sauce.

13. ☐ If / ☐ When } I have enough money I am going to buy champagne.

14. ☐ If / ☐ When } I have another drink I will have to order a taxi.

15. ☐ If / ☐ When } we have finished eating, I am going to have a cigar.

24

Car hire

Lesen Sie die Annonce einer Autovermietungsfirma und beantworten Sie die folgenden zehn Fragen.

1. Are the offers valid for a hire from 13th March to 27th March? ....
2. How much is an Austin Maestro 1.3L?

   ....
3. What is the phone number to call in Canada?

   ....
4. What does a phone call in Canada cost?

   ....
5. Which car is a big family car?

   ....
6. Do the cars have AA breakdown insurance cover?

   ....
7. Is tax (VAT) extra? ....
8. What do you pay for delivery of the car if you fly from Heathrow? ....
9. Can I book 24 hours a day? ....
10. Which car/s is/are advertised in two models?

    ....

LOW SEASON SENSATION

on any rental commencing between
15 JAN and 15 MAR

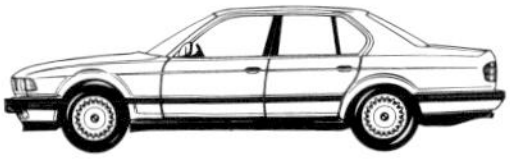

MODEL	
Nissan Micra 1000 (3-door)	£ 66
Austin Maestro 1.3L	£ 76
Austin Montego 2.0HL	£ 124
Peugot 505 Family Est.	£ 199
Ford Granada 2.8i GHIA	£ 269
Rover Vitesse 3500	£ 309
Fiat UNO (5-door)	£ 71
Austin Montego 1.6L	£ 104
Ford Escort XR3i	£ 139
Ford Granada 2.0i	£ 184
Ford Scorpio	£ 281
Rolls Royce Silver Shadow	£ 540

FREE delivery and collection on all rentals to Heathrow, Gatwick airports, Central London, Prestwick, Edinburgh, Glasgow and Manchester.

- **All weekly rates**
- **Full AA breakdown cover**
- **All rates plus VAT 17.5%**
- **Special 4Ks Car Hire Card after first rental**

To reserve your car phone:
USA 800-KAR HIRE CANADA (416) 673-6690 call collect
MIDDLE EAST DUBAI 571891

4Ks CAR HIRE
PO BOX 27 Bracknell, Berks
Tel. 0711-865524 or Fax. 0711-865523
24 hours

25

House and furniture

Hier zur Abwechslung einmal ein Kreuzworträtsel. Alle Wörter kommen aus dem Bereich „Wohnen".

Waagerecht:

1. The young ones play and sleep here.
5. You find this in a British housing block.
6. Where you eat.
7. The top of the house.
8. You have this on most doors.
12. You find this in American housing blocks.
13. Settee or couch.
14. From which the other rooms lead off.
16. You put these small carpets on the floor to keep it clean.
17. Place for sleeping and a good place for pillow fights!

Senkrecht:

1. You put your picture books or afternoon tea on this.
2. You turn it on for music and news.
3. You use it to grow your plants in.
4. A comfortable seat.
9. You put your clothes or your dishes in these.
10. You hang your clothes in here.
11. You put this on the floor to wipe your shoes.
15. Let there be light!

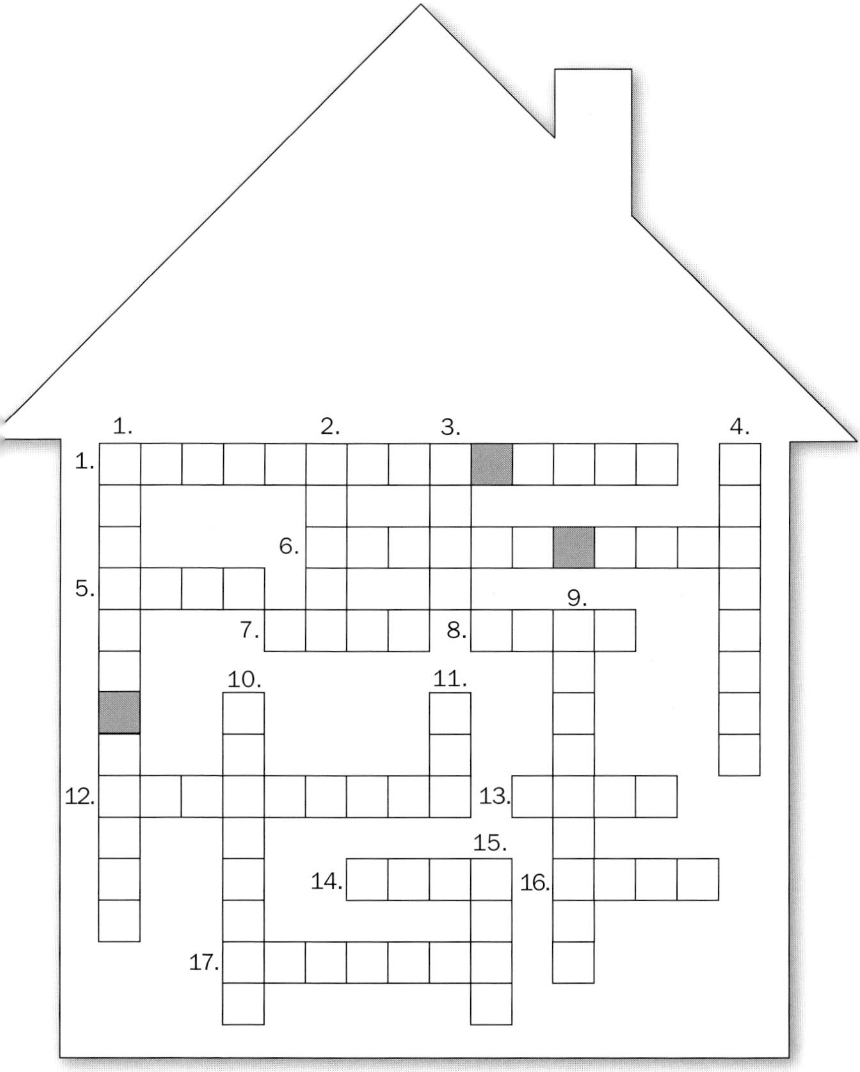
1.
2.
3.
4.
1.
6.
5.
9.
7.
8.
10.
11.
12.
13.
15.
14.
16.
17.

26

Did you know? (2)

Wie gut kennen Sie sich in Großbritannien und den USA aus? Kreuzen Sie an, ob die folgenden Aussagen richtig R *oder falsch* F *sind.*

1. ☐ In Britain a pantomime is a kind of play that has song and dance. The main boy or man character is played by a girl actor and there is always an old woman who is played by a man dressed up.

2. ☐ At a wedding a bride should have four things with her for luck: something old, something new, something borrowed and something blue.

3. ☐ Each country in the UK has a flower as a symbol. The Scottish have the thistle.

4. ☐ The Statue of Liberty was a present from France and is on Ellis Island.

5. ☐ At midnight on New Year's Eve it is traditional for people to hold hands together and sing an old Scottish song.

6. ☐ The UK flag is often called the Union Jack.

7. ☐ "Fish and chips" is a traditional meal to have as a take-away in Britain. Usually it is eaten with salt and vinegar on it.

8. ☐ In the USA a person who enjoys sitting in front of the TV drinking beer and eating crisps is often called a "couch potato."

9. ☐ At Christmas the British eat Christmas pudding. Traditionally it used to have money hidden in it.

27

American clothing

Links finden Sie die amerikanischen, rechts die britischen Bezeichnungen für Kleidungsstücke und Alltagsgegenstände. Ordnen Sie die Wörter richtig zu.

American English

1. ☐ undershirt
2. ☐ pants
3. ☐ robe
4. ☐ tennis shoes
5. ☐ vest
6. ☐ galloshes/rubber boots
7. ☐ pantyhose
8. ☐ nylons
9. ☐ sweater
10. ☐ purse
11. ☐ billfold
12. ☐ raincoat

British English

a) pumps/plimsoles

b) wallet

c) jumper

d) handbag

e) Macintosh

f) stockings

g) vest

h) dressing gown

i) trousers

j) waistcoat

k) tights

l) Wellingtons

28

In the restaurant

Vervollständigen Sie die folgenden Bedingungssätze mit „will“ oder „would“.

1. If the strawberries are fresh I .... eat some.

2. If the fish were local I .... order it.

3. Unless the waiter comes soon I .... leave.

4. If the steak is Argentinian beef I .... try it.

5. If the service was better I .... recommend this restaurant to my friends.

6. Unless the wine is Italian I .... not order a bottle.

7. If the restaurant looked cleaner I .... eat there.

8. If the waiter were French I .... ask him to recommend a good wine.

9. Unless you eat all your vegetables I

   .... not order you any ice cream.

10. As long as you all agree I .... pay the bill.

11. Provided you agree I .... order coffee for us all.

29

Odd word out

In jeder Reihe passt eines der vier Wörter nicht so richtig zu den anderen. Unterstreichen Sie es.

1. office block ● penthouse ● semi-detached house ● block of flats
2. settee ● couch ● sofa ● chair
3. biro ● ball pen ● pencil ● paintbrush
4. car ● lorry ● van ● tanker
5. tent ● B & B ● guest house ● hotel
6. picture ● poster ● photograph ● film
7. dog ● cat ● canary ● chicken
8. croc ● hippo ● elephant ● rhino
9. orange ● potato ● pea ● bean
10. bell ● lights ● brakes ● pump

11. bottle opener ● spoon ● fork ● knife

12. lane ● path ● road ● motorway

13. Mercedes ● BMW ● Porsche ● Morgan

14. red ● yellow ● blue ● green

15. monitor ● keyboard ● cassette ● printer

30

Once upon a time ...

Ergänzen Sie das folgende Märchen mit den Verben aus dem Kasten.

called • surprised • went • demanded
ran • met • answered • did • turned
wanted • decided • found • dressed
dropped • gave • felt • explained
had • said

Once upon a time there was a rich king who had a servant .... ❶ Thomas. One morning Thomas was at the market buying fresh fruit and vegetables. All at once he .... ❷ a strange feeling and he .... ❸ very cold. He .... ❹ round and saw a tall man .... ❺ all in black behind him. He asked the man who he was and the man .... ❻ "My name is Death."

Thomas .... ❼ his basket of fruit and vegetables and .... ❽ to the king. He asked the king if he could have two or three days extra holiday. The king was very puzzled and asked Thomas if anything was wrong. Thomas .... (9) that he had .... (10) Death in the market and he .... (11) to leave the town and visit his aunt in Manchester. The king could see that Thomas was very frightened and .... (12) him permission to have two days off.

The king was a very wise man and .... (13) to find out more about the strange visitor. He .... (14) to the market and .... (15) the stranger. He went up to him and said, "Who are you?" The stranger ...., (16) "I am Death." The king ...., (17) "Why .... (18) you frighten my servant Thomas?" "Who is your servant?" replied the stranger. "My servant is Thomas," said the king. "I was very .... (19) to see Thomas." "Why?" asked the king. "Because I have an appointment with Thomas tomorrow night in Manchester," said the stranger.

31

False friends (2)

Sind Sie auf die folgenden „falschen Freunde" auch schon einmal hereingefallen? Dann schreiben Sie jetzt die richtige Übersetzung neben jedes Wort.

1. to become ....
   bekommen ....

2. card ....
   Karte ....

3. chef ....
   Chef ....

4. to concern ....
   Konzern ....

5. gift ....
   Gift ....

6. map ....
   Mappe ....

7. menu ....
   Menü ....

8. prospect ....
   Prospekt ....

9. receipt ....
   Rezept ....

10. stream ....
    Strom ....

11. eventually ....
    eventuell ....

12. gymnasium ....
    Gymnasium ....

13. pension ....
    Pension ....

14. sensible ....
    sensibel ....

15. warehouse ....
    Warenhaus ....

32

The car

Benennen Sie die verschiedenen Autoteile.

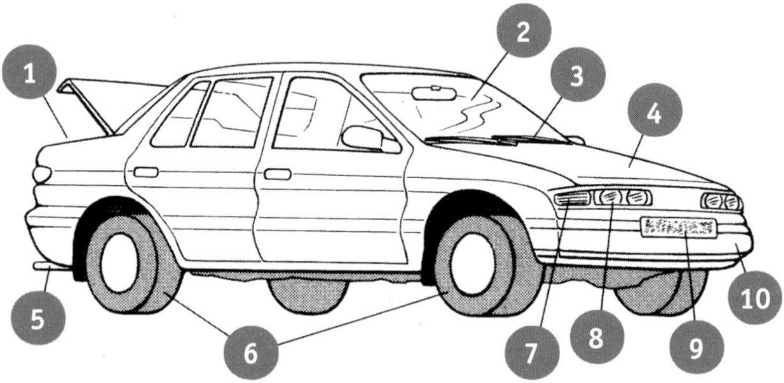

1 ....

2 ....

3 ....

4 ....

5 ....

6 ....

7 ....

8 ....

9 ....

10 ....

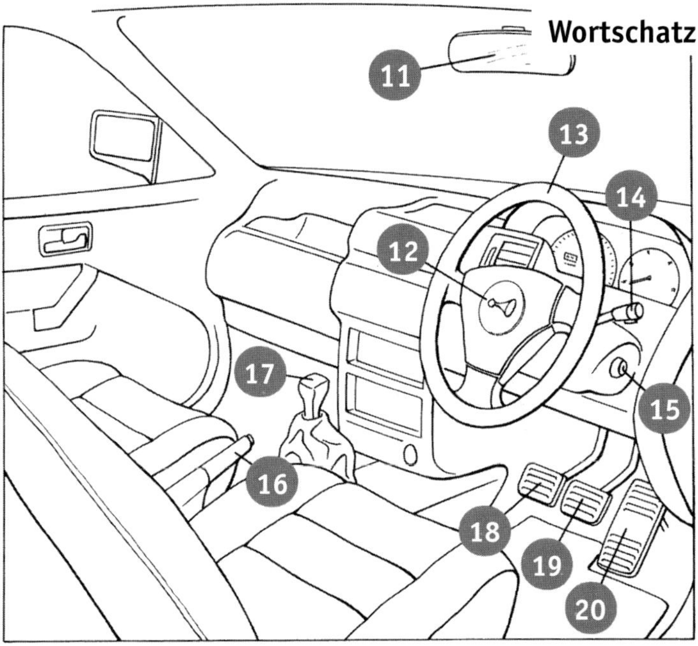

11 ....

12 ....

13 ....

14 ....

15 ....

16 ....

17 ....

18 ....

19 ....

20 ....

21 ....

22 ....

33

Now or never

Unterstreichen Sie in den folgenden Sätzen die richtige Gegenwartsform: simple present oder present progressive.

1. I work/am working for an electronics company in Manchester.
2. Paul is playing/plays tennis every Friday evening.
3. In my spare time I am reading/read a lot.
4. Barbara's plane is leaving/leaves Heathrow at 10.15 tomorrow.
5. The English course is starting/starts on September 5th.
6. I can't come with you yet, I am playing/play table football at the moment.
7. Look at that man! He is trying/tries to climb into that garden.
8. I live/am living in Staines, it is a town near London.
9. The bus we have hired leaves/is leaving at 6 a.m. so don't be late.
10. The concert is quite long, it lasts/is lasting three hours.

11. I do/am doing my homework. I'll be done in a few minutes.

12. Catherine is writing/writes all her letters on her computer.

13. David is travelling/travels to Stockholm once a month on business.

14. The journey takes/is taking three hours by train and two by car.

15. My parents shop/are out shopping now. I'll tell them you phoned.

34

Correct response (2)

Nicht alle vier Antworten auf die folgenden Fragen sind richtig. Kreuzen Sie die möglichen Antworten an.

1. What was the film like?
   - ☐ a) Very good.
   - ☐ b) Super, one of the best I've seen.
   - ☐ c) A bit like the theatre but not with real people.
   - ☐ d) A bit like Dr Zhivago but shorter.

2. Goodbye.
   - ☐ a) Bye.
   - ☐ b) Sooner or later.
   - ☐ c) Be seeing you.
   - ☐ d) Until next time.

3. Are you married?
   - ☐ a) Yes.
   - ☐ b) No, I'm a single person.
   - ☐ c) No, I'm divorced.
   - ☐ d) With three children.

4. Would you like a drink?
   - ☐ a) Yes, I'd love a soft drink.
   - ☐ b) Yes, I like beer.
   - ☐ c) No, thank you.
   - ☐ d) Good idea.

5. Can I help you?
   - ☐ a) No, I'm just looking.
   - ☐ b) Yes, please.
   - ☐ c) Have you got this pullover in a larger size?
   - ☐ d) Yes, I'd be glad to.

6. How much is it?
   - ☐ a) Seventy-five pence a kilo.
   - ☐ b) Twenty pence.
   - ☐ c) Very expensive.
   - ☐ d) Three pounds per packet.

7. Do you like tennis?
   - ☐ a) I'd love to.
   - ☐ b) I love it.
   - ☐ c) I'm crazy about it.
   - ☐ d) It's my favourite sport.

8. What time do you have breakfast?
   - ☐ a) Seven-twenty.
   - ☐ b) Ten minutes before half past seven.
   - ☐ c) Twenty past seven.
   - ☐ d) Twenty minutes after seven.

9. How do you start the day?
   - ☐ a) I get up at six-thirty.
   - ☐ b) I stand up at six-thirty.
   - ☐ c) I get out of bed at six-thirty.
   - ☐ d) I climb out of bed at six-thirty.

10. That's a nice picture. What do you think?
   - ☐ a) I mean it's very pretty.
   - ☐ b) I think it's very ugly.
   - ☐ c) I don't like it at all.
   - ☐ d) In my opinion it's terrible.

35

Hopping mad

Lesen Sie den folgenden Artikel und kennzeichnen Sie anschließend die Aussagen auf der rechten Seite mit [R] *für richtig oder* [F] *für falsch.*

Hopping mad

To be hopping mad is to be very angry about something. To hop is to jump up and down like a kangaroo. Farmer Hans-Ulrich Hege of Schwäbisch Hall was hopping mad a couple of years ago when rabbits and hares started hopping into his farm and eating all the young plants in his fields.

Mr Hege is growing a new variety of lupins for cows to eat and the new variety tastes sweeter so the rabbits were eating the plants in large numbers. He tried all sorts of ways to keep the animals out, such as fences, sirens and poison but nothing worked.

Mr Hege is a very clever person and not afraid to try old-fashioned ideas. He got his friends to collect the hair that they had on their brushes and combs. He put this on the ground around the flowers that he had planted.

The treatment was 100% effective. The method is environmentally friendly and causes the animals no harm. Mr Hege thinks that the smell is too strong for the rabbits and perhaps they do not like the smell of soap and shampoo which is on the hair. Now the rabbits are hopping mad!

1. ☐ Mr Hege lives in Britain.
2. ☐ He had problems with kangaroos.
3. ☐ He tried different methods to keep the animals away.
4. ☐ Mr Hege only uses very modern methods.
5. ☐ His friends told him what to do.
6. ☐ He grows lupins for sale in flower shops.
7. ☐ He put brushes and combs on the ground.
8. ☐ The rabbits and hares liked the smell.
9. ☐ The hair killed the rabbits.
10. ☐ Mr Hege is now hopping mad.

36

Simple past or past progressive?

Unterstreichen Sie in der folgenden Geschichte die richtige Vergangenheitsform: simple past oder past progressive .

1. Joe and I had/were having a terrible experience on holiday last week.

2. When we arrived at our holiday cottage we found/were finding out that it was near the sea, as advertised, but it was five kilometres from the nearest town.

3. So we had to hire a car. The car we got was a very modern four-door that looked sporty. The next morning as we were driving/drove to town the motor stopped at a set of traffic lights.

4. So Joe and I were pushing/pushed it up the road, which was on a little hill, and tried to start it. Unfortunately we did not notice the little tree at the side of the road.

5. All at once the car started rolling back. As it was rolling/rolled down the hill the driver's door hit the tree and made a loud noise before falling off.

6. We were telephoning/telephoned the car hire service and they sent a replacement car; this was an older car and a little bit rusty, but it started first time.

7. That afternoon we drove/were driving to a beach about half an hour away and we had a nice time.

8. Just as we got back/were getting back to the car park, our rusty old car disappeared around the corner; it had been stolen!

9. We telephoned the car hire people again and they were very nice and said they were insured, but Joe and I hired/were hiring two bicycles after that.

10. However, as we were riding/rode into town yesterday we both had punctures and needed to repair the tyres.
    We have decided not to hire a car or bicycles next time we go on holiday!

37

Train travel

Sehen Sie sich den Auszug aus dem Zugfahrplan genau an und beantworten Sie die folgenden Fragen.

1. What time must I leave Paddington to arrive in Plymouth before 12 o'clock? ....
2. How many trains arrive in Exeter before 2 p.m.?

   ....
3. Which train from Paddington arrives in Penzance at 22.50? ....
4. If I leave Westbury at 15.27 what time will I arrive in Newton Abbot? ....
5. Can I travel this route on Friday? ....
6. How many trains are special Friday trains?

   ....
7. What must I do if I want to travel on the 10.50 from Paddington? ....
8. How many trains travel straight through from Paddington to Paignton on the "English Riviera"?

   ....
9. Which train from Paddington does not provide hot meals? ....

MONDAYS TO FRIDAYS

		◇	◇	◇	R ◇	◇	◇	◇	◇	◇	◇	◇	◇	◇	◇	◇	◇
		A			E			FX	FO	FO		A		D	FO	FO	FX
		125	125	125	125		125	125	125		125	125	125	125	125	125	125
		⊘	⊘	⊘	⊘	⊘	⊘	⊘	⊘		⊘	⊘	⊘	⊘	⊘	⊘	⊘
London Paddington	d	07 25	08 50	10 10	10 50	11 45	12 45	14 15	14 30	14 35	15 45	16 05	16 45	17 45	18 40	19 00	19 00
Reading	d	07 53	09 16	10 36	—	12 17	13 11	14 41	14 59	15 07	16 11	16 30u	17 10u	18 10u	—	19 25u	19 25u
Westbury	a	08 04	10 05	11 23	—	—	14 00	15 27	—	16 00	—	—	18 00	—	19 49	—	20 16
Castle Cary	a	—	—	—	—	—	—	—	—	—	—	—	18 19	—	—	20 28	20 34
Taunton	a	09 44	10 45	12 02	—	13 47	14 40	16 05	—	16 41	17 32	18 33	18 43	19 27	20 27	20 52	20 57
Tiverton Parkway	a	—	10 59	12 16	—	—	—	16 18	16 25	—	—	—	18 57	—	—	21 06	21 11
Exeter St David's	a	10 12	11 16	12 33	12 50	14 21	15 10	16 35	16 42	17 13	18 00	19 01	19 14	19 55	20 55	21 23	21 27
Exeter St David's	d	10 13	11 16	12 34	13 20	14 28	15 12	16 36	16 47	17 15	18 00	19 01	19 16	19 56	20 55	21 24	21 29
Newton Abbot	a	10 34	11 37	12 59	13 50	15 00	15 33	16 57	17 23	17 40	18 21	19 26	—	20 17	—	21 45	21 50
Newton Abbot	d	10 54	11 45	—	13 52	15 15	16 03	17 24	17 24	18 02	18 48	19 28	19 37	20 25	—	21 55	21 55
Torquay	a	11 04	11 55	—	14 03	15 25	16 14	17 35	17 35	18 13	18 58	19 40	—	20 35	—	22 05	22 05
Paignton	a	11 11	12 01	—	14 09	15 32	16 20	17 42	17 42	18 20	19 04	19 48	—	20 41	—	22 11	22 11
Totnes	a	—	11 51	13 13	—	—	15 47	17 11	—	17 56	—	—	19 51	20 58	—	21 59	22 04
Plymouth	a	11 14	12 21	13 43	13 50	15 27	16 17	17 41	17 40	18 27	19 01	—	20 21	20 57	21 53	22 29	22 35
Plymouth	d	11 17	—	—	13 53	15 35	16 35	17 44	17 44	—	19 04	—	—	21 00	—	22 32	—
Liskeard	a	11 41	—	—	14 17	16 02	17 10	18 08	18 08	—	19 28	—	—	21 25	—	22 55	—
St Austell	a	12 12	—	—	14 48	16 34	17 45	18 37	18 37	—	20 01	—	—	21 55	—	23 23	—
Truro	a	12 30	—	—	15 06	16 53	18 03	18 55	18 55	—	20 19	—	—	22 13	—	23 41	—
Redruth	a	12 43	—	—	15 19	17 10	18 19	19 08	19 08	—	20 32	—	—	22 26	—	23 53	—
Penzance	a	13 10	—	—	15 46	17 42	18 50	19 32	19 32	—	21 00	—	—	22 50	—	00 14	—

Timetable Notes

A Via Bath Spa
E **Cornish Riviera**
FO Fridays only
FX Fridays excepted
⊘ Hot dishes available to order, or restaurant service of meals. Also buffet service of drinks, hot or cold snacks available for whole or part of journey

R Train in which reservation is compulsory for whole or part of journey for the whole or part of the currency of the timetable.
◇ Seats may be reserved on trains to which this symbol applies
125 Train formed of InterCity 125 stock

38

Music

Hier sind zehn Begriffe zum Thema „Musik“ versteckt. Kreisen Sie sie ein und ordnen Sie sie der passenden Definition zu.

C	X	T	C	S	O	N	G	X
L	G	R	H	I	P	D	A	S
A	G	U	I	T	A	R	V	L
R	Q	M	V	O	K	U	N	Z
I	S	P	H	I	L	M	O	H
N	R	E	C	O	R	D	T	O
E	Y	T	S	I	N	G	E	R
T	V	I	O	L	I	N	S	N

1. Three types of wind instruments for blowing into, two are of brass:

   ....

2. Two types of string instruments:

   ....

3. A piece of music that is sung:

   ....

4. An instrument that you hit:

   ....

5. Symbols for writing music:

   ....

6. A person whose instrument is her/his voice:

   ....

7. Many bands want to make one of these with their music:

   ....

39

Question time

Die folgenden dreizehn Fragen sind durcheinandergeraten. Schreiben Sie sie in der richtigen Reihenfolge auf.

1. mind ● would ● you ● opening ● door ● the

   ....?

2. long ● you ● have ● how ● here ● lived

   ....?

3. buy ● you ● did ● car ● where ● your ● new

   ....?

4. double ● for ● night ● one ● you ● do ● have ● a ● room ....

   ....?

5. information ● could ● town ● some ● you ● me ● give ● about ● this ● please ....

   ....?

6. restaurant ● would ● to ● friends ● you ● your ● this ● recommend ....

   ....?

7. worked ● you ● long ● have ● here ● how

....?

8. did ● fly ● you ● America ● to ● when

....?

9. tennis ● playing ● you ● long ● have ● been ● how ....

....?

10. when ● the ● you ● meet ● for ● did ● first ● wife ● time ● your ....

....?

11. times ● Malta ● you ● how ● have ● been ● many ● to ....

....?

12. cinema ● night ● you ● go ● to ● last ● did ● the ....

....?

13. book ● Grisham ● new ● have ● read ● you ● the ● by ● yet ....

....?

40

At the hospital

In der Schilderung eines Fahrradunfalls sind die Buchstaben einiger Wörter durcheinandergeraten. Wie müssen diese Wörter richtig lauten? Schreiben Sie sie in die Lücken.

Last Saturday I had an accident on my bicycle. I was riding down a steep hill when my brakes failed and I crashed into a car and fell off my bike. I hurt my arm and banged my head. Luckily someone saw the accident and called for an CELANAMBU .... ❶.

Very soon it arrived and two men climbed out with a TCHRESTRE .... ❷, which they quickly put me on to. As we were driving to the LOSPIHAT .... ❸ one of the men gave me an JETCIOINN .... ❹.

As soon as we arrived I was handed over to a young RUNSE .... ❺, who wiped away the DOBLO .... ❻ from my face and arm. She also gave me a BLATTE .... ❼ which she said was to make the pain less.

Soon a DROOCT .... ❽ came and said that they would have to PEROTEA .... ❾ as my arm was broken.

When I woke up some hours later I had a large SPLATER .... ❿ on my arm and a BNADAGE .... ⓫ on my head. I was given some more DEMINICE .... ⓬ and two days later was allowed to go home.

41

Where am I?

A

Hier kommt es auf Ihr Allgemeinwissen und die richtige Schreibweise der Länder an. Schreiben Sie das Land neben die jeweilige Hauptstadt. Was ergibt sich senkrecht?

1. Lima
2. Cairo
3. Bucharest
4. Taipeh
5. Budapest

6. Vienna
7. Washington, D.C.
8. Stockholm
9. Bangkok
10. Kigali
11. Tirana
12. Beirut
13. Rome
14. Buenos Aires

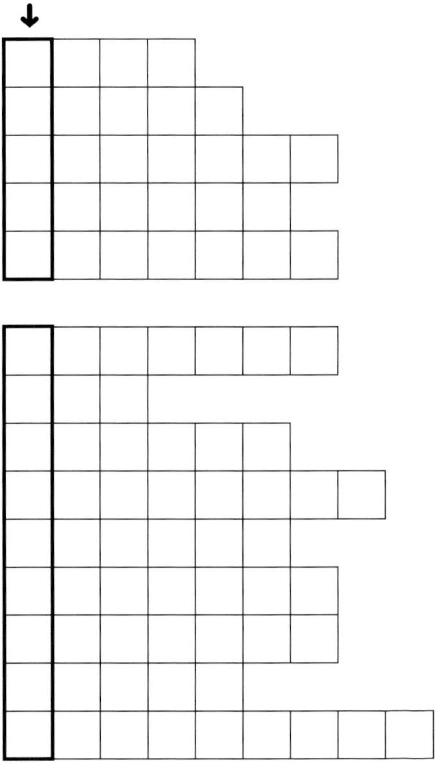

B

Schreiben Sie auch hier das Land neben die jeweilige Währung. Welches Land erhalten Sie senkrecht?

1. Yuan
2. Euro
3. Krona

4. SFranc
5. Peso
6. Real
7. Tolar
8. Lev
9. Forint
10. Rupee

42

Opposites

Suchen Sie das Gegenteil zu den fett gedruckten Wörtern.

1. **little** house ....
2. **back** garden ....
3. **empty** glass ....
4. **happy** person ....
5. **easy** question ....
6. **hot** day ....
7. **dark** room ....
8. **open** suitcase ....
9. **fast** car ....
10. **high** shelf ....

11. **ugly** person ....

12. **good** person ....

13. **old** building ....

14. **wet** towel ....

15. **clean** child ....

16. **heavy** suitcase ....

17. **long** hair ....

18. **strong** metal ....

19. **fat** politician ....

20. **sharp** knife ....

43

Ferry travel

Lesen Sie den folgenden Text und füllen Sie danach das Formular aus.

It was hot on that first day of August 2006 as Harry Hallen, a hired killer who told his wife he was a car salesman, drove his 318i BMW onto the ferry.

He had bought himself a personalized number plate with his initials and the same number as the car. He could have got one with his age on, but he did not want people to know it was his fiftieth birthday next year. 'Half a ton,' he thought to himself. He had earned this holiday with his wife, Kathy, and the two kids, Benjamin and Barbara.

He had been looking forward to his holiday in Scotland since booking it in April. They were on their way to a holiday house in the Highlands. Strangely the house in Scotland had the same address as their flat in Munich if you translated it directly: 7 Queen's Road. But the postcode was different. In Munich it was 80539.

Harry liked driving but was a little nervous about the ferry trip as he often got seasick. This was his first contract in Britain. He was looking forward to seeing Queen Elizabeth II at the annual Highland Games!

FERRY BOARDING CARD

Name: ....

Address: ....

Postcode: ....

Your Age: 18-30 31–40 41-50 50+

1. How are you travelling:

   Foot Car Coach Freight

2. If travelling by car, what is the make of your car?

   Make (eg Ford) .... Model (eg Sierra) ....

   Registration No ....

3. What is your final destination? ....

4. What is the purpose of your journey?

   Touring Camping/caravan Skiing

   Resort/City stay Weekend break Day trip

5. When did you book your crossing? Month........... 20 ....

6. Are you Single Married

7. Do you have any children? yes no

8. What is your occupation? ....

44

Flying tonight

Suchen Sie die folgenden Begriffe, die alle aus dem Bereich des Fliegens kommen, und tragen Sie sie in die entsprechende Zeile ein. Die grauen Kästchen verraten Ihnen (senkrecht gelesen), an welchem Ort man Menschen aus vielen verschiedenen Ländern treffen kann.

1. This is often filled with hot air or gas.
2. Children should not fly this near an airport.
3. You need this to get on an aircraft.
4. Many people stay here overnight before flying.
5. Each plane has at least one and some have four.
6. This gets you off the ground.
7. This aircraft has no motor.
8. The aircraft lands and takes off on this.
9. When you fly you are one.
10. The person who flies the plane.
11. Another word for journey, especially when on business.
12. The person who takes care of you.

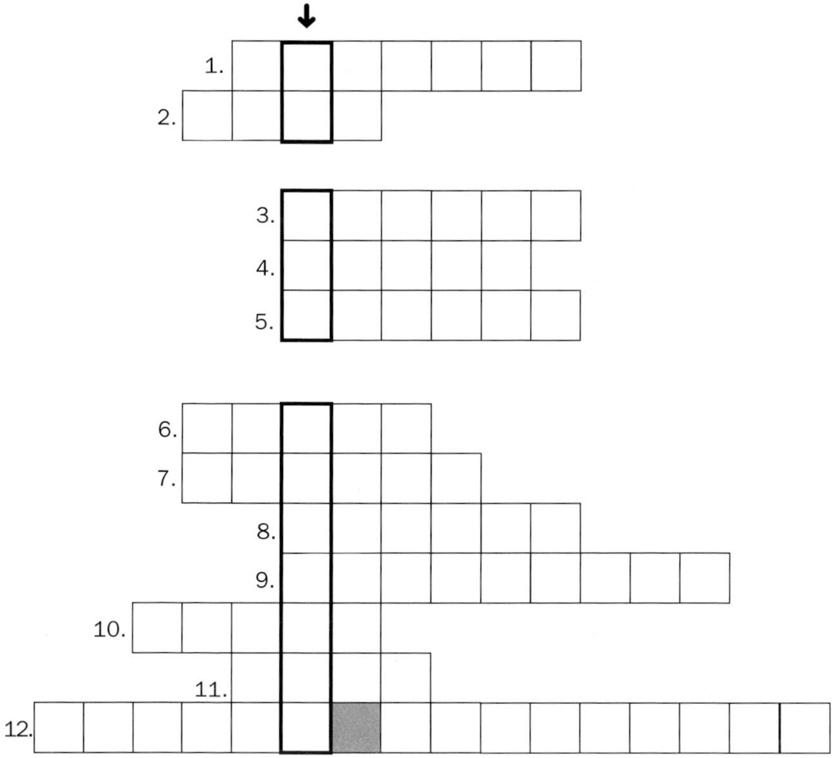
1.
2.
3.
4.
5.
6.
7.
8.
9.
10.
11.
12.

45

“Stealing” or “to steal”?

Unterstreichen Sie, ob der Infinitiv oder die -ing-Form richtig ist.

1. The thief admitted stealing/to steal the car.
2. We considered going/to go to the ballet, but the tickets were too expensive.
3. They decided going/to go to the cinema.
4. We enjoyed staying/to stay with my parents-in-law on holiday.
5. Would you mind shutting/to shut the window, please?
6. After the party the couple needed going/to go for a walk to clear their heads.
7. My mother offered looking/to look after the children next weekend if we want.
8. The workers were prepared working/to work overtime if it was necessary.
9. Sally recommended visiting/to visit the museum in the afternoon.
10. Somebody suggested calling/to call round at my brother’s house.

11. The children all wanted eating/to eat an ice cream.

12. Sue wished travelling/to travel to America before she died.

13. She stopped smoking/to smoke when she had to go to hospital.

14. He began jogging/to jog when he was 36.

15. He stopped smoking/to smoke his pipe after he had written the fourth letter.

46

At the zoo

A

In dieser Schlange sind zwanzig Tiernamen versteckt. Der letzte Buchstabe des einen Tieres ist auch der Anfangsbuchstabe des nächsten. Kreisen Sie die Wörter ein.

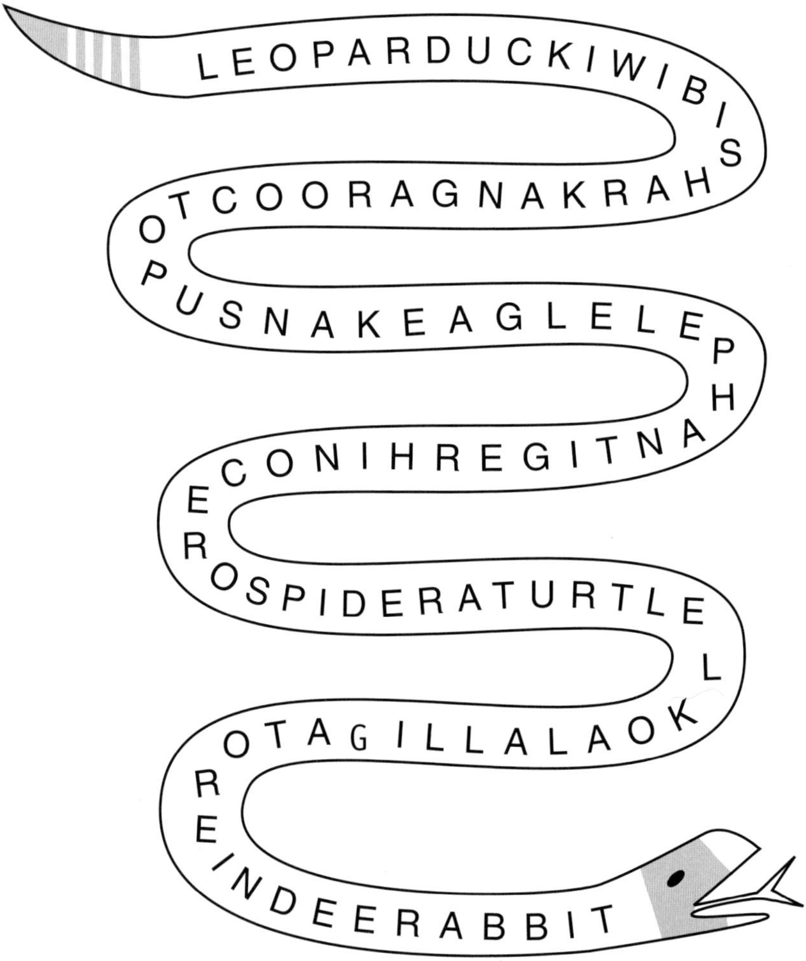

B

Versuchen Sie nun, die folgenden Tiere und ihre Jungen einander zuzuordnen.

1.	☐ cat	a)	piglet
2.	☐ dog	b)	leveret
3.	☐ cow	c)	cub
4.	☐ sheep	d)	goslet
5.	☐ bird	e)	cygnet
6.	☐ goose	f)	puppy
7.	☐ swan	g)	fledgeling
8.	☐ rabbit	h)	kitten
9.	☐ tiger	i)	lamb
10.	☐ pig	j)	calf

47

How long have you been here?

Kreuzen Sie die richtige Übersetzung für den deutschen Satz an. (Nur einer der drei Sätze ist richtig.)

1. Er arbeitet seit vier Jahren bei uns.
   a) ☐ He has worked for us for four years.
   b) ☐ He is working for us for four years.
   c) ☐ He has worked for us since four years.

2. Seit einigen Jahren leben wir im Raum Stuttgart.
   a) ☐ We have been living in the Stuttgart area for a number of years.
   b) ☐ We have been living in the Stuttgart area since a number of years.
   c) ☐ We are living in the Stuttgart area for a number of years.

3. Ich hatte gestern einen Unfall.
   a) ☐ I had an accident yesterday.
   b) ☐ I have had an accident yesterday.
   c) ☐ Yesterday I have had an accident.

4. Als Kind habe ich Tennis gespielt.
   a) ☐ I played tennis when I was young.
   b) ☐ I have played tennis when I was young.
   c) ☐ I have played tennis since I was young.

5. Ich habe meine Frau vor 20 Jahren kennen gelernt.
   a) ☐ I have met my wife twenty years ago.
   b) ☐ I have met my wife for twenty years.
   c) ☐ I met my wife twenty years ago.

6. Seit Weihnachten ist sie Personalchefin.
   a) ☐ She has been the Personnel Manager since Christmas.
   b) ☐ She is the Personnel Manager since Christmas.
   c) ☐ She has been my personal manager since Christmas.

7. Sie kennen sich seit fast zehn Jahren.
   a) ☐ They are knowing each other for ten years.
   b) ☐ They have known each other for nearly ten years.
   c) ☐ They know each other for ten years.

8. Wir haben letzte Woche einen Hund gekauft.
   a) ☐ We bought a dog last week.
   b) ☐ We have bought a dog last week.
   c) ☐ We have bought a dog since last week.

9. Ich habe dieses Auto seit zwei Jahren.
   a) ☐ I have had this car for two years.
   b) ☐ I have this car for two years.
   c) ☐ I had this car for two years.

48

Kidnapping

Lesen Sie zuerst die Aussagen, dann den Zeitungsartikel und kennzeichnen Sie anschließend, ob die Aussagen richtig R *oder falsch* F *sind.*

1. ☐ The family had been to watch car racing.
2. ☐ The boy was sixteen.
3. ☐ The car was a Vauxhall Cavalier.
4. ☐ The family were from Cornwall.
5. ☐ The car stopped at a bus stop to let the boy out of the boot.
6. ☐ A man phoned the police.
7. ☐ The car was stopped quarter of an hour after the phone call.
8. ☐ The family had tried to save money.
9. ☐ The family were taken to a police station.
10. ☐ Putting someone in the boot could be dangerous.

Kidnapping

A kidnap alert was started when a woman saw a teenager being put in the boot of a car. But it turned out that it was his own parents who had put him in the back to avoid having to pay for him to get into the horse races at Newton Abbot race course.

The woman spotted a blue Vauxhall Cavalier when it pulled up at a bus stop. She watched as the driver got out of the car and opened the boot with a boy of about 17 inside. The woman took the number of the car and telephoned the police thinking that she had seen a kidnapping. The police were alerted and the car was stopped about half an hour later as it was crossing into Cornwall – only five minutes from their home. They looked in the boot but there was no one in it. However, there was a young boy of 16 sitting in the car. The driver and his wife were taken to a police station and questioned. The driver explained that getting into the races was very expensive and to avoid paying for the boy they had put him in the back of the car. When leaving the races they thought that the boy would be seen so they had hidden him in the boot for a second time.

The police warned other families that this was a very dangerous thing to do and that the boy could have died if left in the boot of the car for too long.

49

Booking a room

Hier ist ein Gespräch zwischen einer Hotelrezeptionistin (🗨) und einem Gast (🗩) durcheinandergeraten. Nummerieren Sie die richtige Reihenfolge in den Kästchen.

☐ 🗩 Does that include breakfast?

☐ 🗨 Fine. If you'd just like to fill this in, I'll get you your key.

☐ 🗩 Good evening. I'd like a room.

☐ 🗩 And does it have a bath or shower?

☐ 🗩 Thank you.

☐ 🗨 Yes Sir, it does. Continental.

☐ 🗨 A double or a single, Sir?

- [ ] Good evening. Can I help you?

- [ ] Yes, that's fine. How much is it?

- [ ] OK. I'll take it.

- [ ] Yes, Sir. The lift is over there in the corner.

- [ ] I'd like a double room please.
At the front if possible.

- [ ] Yes, OK. Oh, one last question.
Is there a lift?

- [ ] It has a shower and a toilet.
Is that suitable?

- [ ] Yes, Sir. We have a double on the fourth floor.

- [ ] It's £ 45 per night.

50

One and one makes ...

Schreiben Sie neben die folgenden Wörter deren Mehrzahl, sofern es eine Pluralform gibt.

1. sheep ....
2. fish ....
3. child ....
4. hair ....
5. deer ....
6. toy ....
7. woman ....
8. dog ....
9. data ....
10. cactus ....

11. advice ....
12. book ....
13. man ....
14. record ....
15. news ....
16. grass ....
17. information ....
18. beer ....
19. person ....
20. coffee ....

Lösungen

1

A

1. **... White Hart – a bunch of flowers arranged in a heart shape.** *White Hart* ist ein häufiger Name für Pubs. Ein *hart* ist ein *Hirsch*. Das Motiv auf dem Schild müsste also einen weißen Hirsch zeigen. Das *Herz (heart)* wird allerdings genauso ausgesprochen.
2. **... and he came over to me to ask what I wanted to drink.** Wer in einem typisch britischen Pub am Tisch wartet, bis jemand die Bestellung aufnimmt, wartet vergebens. Bestellt wird direkt *an der Theke (at the bar)* und für jedes Getränk wird immer sofort bezahlt.
3. **... half a litre of beer.** In Großbritannien wird Bier immer noch im *pint* bestellt, das entspricht etwa 0,57 Litern. Die nächstkleinere Einheit wäre *half-a-pint*.
4. **... a shelf where the daily paper is kept ...** Es ist in einem Pub nicht üblich, dass für die Gäste eine Zeitung ausliegt.
5. **... so I ordered a bottle of white wine.** Eine ganze Flasche Wein bestellt im Pub kaum jemand. Vielleicht liegt es am relativ hohen Preis. Es ist zwar möglich, ein Glas Wein zu trinken, das Standardgetränk ist allerdings Bier.
6. **... for the three of us and we began to play bridge.** Bridge ist ein sehr beliebtes Kartenspiel, es wird allerdings kaum jemals in Pubs gespielt. Im Übrigen braucht man für eine Partie Bridge vier Spieler/innen.
7. **... I had lost some money.** Beim Bridge wird grundsätzlich nicht um Geld gespielt. In Pubs ist zwar Kartenspielen um Geld erlaubt, allerdings ist gesetzlich geregelt, wie hoch die Einsätze sein dürfen.
8. **... I asked for the bill, paid and walked home.** Im Pub zahlt man jedes Getränk sofort, wenn man es an der Theke holt (siehe 1). Wenn man mit Bekannten, Kollegen oder Kolleginnen im Pub ist, ist es üblich, dass jeder einmal eine Runde zahlt *(This round's on me.)*.

B

1. **f**
2. **a**
3. **e**

4. **d**
5. **h**; Kurzform für *ploughman's lunch*, wird nur zur Mittagszeit serviert.
6. **c**
7. **b**
8. **g**

Tipp

Es ist nicht üblich, im Pub Trinkgeld zu geben. Wenn Sie die Person hinter der Theke *(barman/barwoman)* kennen, können Sie jedoch Geld im Werte eines Getränks anbieten: *Would you like one for yourself?*

2

T	O	Y	S	F	S	D	V
O	F	G	S	H	O	E	S
W	S	C	U	S	A	Z	W
E	S	N	N	F	P	J	I
L	U	K	G	C	M	C	M
A	I	L	L	V	N	A	S
X	T	B	A	L	L	M	U
H	C	K	S	N	M	E	I
P	A	S	S	P	O	R	T
L	S	H	E	S	W	A	D
O	E	B	S	D	T	F	C

1. **towel.** Es gibt Handtücher, die man mit an den Strand nimmt *(beach towels)*, kleinere für die Hände *(hand towels)* und Geschirrtücher *(tea towels)*.
2. **toys**
3. **suitcase.** Nicht zu verwechseln mit *briefcase (Aktentasche)*.

4. **sunglasses.** Sie werden im Amerikanischen auch *shades* genannt.
5. **ball**
6. **camera**
7. **passport.** Britische Staatsangehörige brauchen nur einen Pass, wenn sie ins Ausland reisen möchten. Innerhalb von Großbritannien gibt es (noch) keine Ausweispflicht.
8. **swimsuit.** Synonyme wären auch *swimming trunks* für „Ihn" oder *swimming costume* für „Sie".
9. **soap**
10. **shoes**

Tipp

Das englische Wort für *Ferien* ist *holiday* und kommt vom altenglischen *holy day* (heiliger Tag). An diesem Tag wurde nicht gearbeitet. Das Wort *holiday* wird hauptsächlich in Großbritannien für *Ferien/Urlaub* verwendet, in den USA sagt man *vacation* dazu.

Übrigens: Wussten Sie schon, woher das Wort *soap opera* kommt? Den Namen bekamen fortlaufende Fernsehserien, weil sie so trivial waren wie die Werbespots für Seife.

3

1. **for** 15 years. *For* bezieht sich in der Regel auf eine Zeitdauer, hier 15 Jahre.
2. **for** 13 years
3. **since** 1985. *Since* bezieht sich in der Regel auf einen Zeitpunkt in der Vergangenheit, hier 1985.
4. **for** 19 years
5. **since** our daughters started at the same kindergarten. In den USA ist das Wort *kindergarten* üblich, in Großbritannien sagt man *playgroup* oder *playschool*.
6. **since** January 1992
7. **since** August last year
8. **for** six years
9. **for** many years. Von *fanatic* kommt übrigens das deutsche Wort *Fan*.
10. **since** then, d. h. als sie den Film sah.

Tipp

Skittles ist die britische Entsprechung zu *Kegeln* und wird oft in Pubs gespielt, wobei Mannschaften gegeneinander antreten. Jede kleine Stadt hat eine Liga (*skittles league*). Die *Kugeln* (*balls*) und die *Kegel* (*skittles*) sind normalerweise aus Holz. Manche *Bahnen* (*lanes*) sind zerlegbar und können nach dem Spiel auseinandergebaut werden.

4

1. **a)**
2. **b)** und **d)** *How do you do?* ist eine Begrüßungsfloskel und keine Frage nach dem Befinden. Die Antworten a) und c) wären auf die Frage *How are you?* richtig.
3. **a)** und **b)**
4. **c)** d) klingt unhöflich.
5. **b)** c) wäre sehr unhöflich.
6. **a)** und **d)** a) passt, wenn es ein Rauchverbot gibt. b) und c) wären zwar sprachlich richtig, aber sehr unhöflich.
7. **a)** und **b)** c) wirkt unhöflich, und d) geht höchstens unter guten Bekannten.
8. **a)** und **c)**
9. **b)** und **d)** Das *Present Perfect* deutet darauf hin, dass die befragte Person noch dort wohnt. Die einfache Vergangenheit in a) ist falsch, denn sie zeigt an, dass die Person früher einmal dort gewohnt hat, jedoch heute nicht mehr. c) geht nicht, weil sich das Verb *stay* nur auf vorübergehende Aufenthalte (z. B. im Hotel) bezieht. *Live* ist hier im Sinne von *wohnen* gemeint.
10. **a)** und **d)** Bei der Frage nach dem Beruf muss die Antwort in der einfachen Vergangenheit stehen. b) und c) wären richtige Antworten auf die Frage *What are you doing?* – *Was tust du gerade?*
11. **c)** Möglich wären auch *That's OK* oder *Not at all* für das kurze deutsche *Bitte(schön)*. *Please* wird nur in Bitten verwendet, z. B. *Can you help me, please?*

Tipp

Im Englischen wirkt es äußerst unhöflich, einfach nur mit *Yes* oder *No* zu antworten. „Verpacken" Sie daher Ihre Antworten in ein paar freundliche Worte. Bei negativen Antworten können Sie z. B. *I'm afraid/I'm sorry/Well …* einbauen.

Aufgepasst bei Fragen, die mit *Would you mind* beginnen: mit der Antwort *No* stimmen Sie zu (*No, I wouldn't mind.*), mit *Yes* lehnen Sie ab. Übrigens: Folgt nach *Would you mind* ein Verb, so muss es in der *ing*- Form stehen, z. B.: *Would you mind opening the window?*

→ Siehe auch Übung 34.

5

1. **do;** *do one's best – sein Bestes tun*
2. **make;** *make a complaint – sich beschweren.* Wenn man von Lebensmitteln sagt, sie seien *off*, so bedeutet das *verdorben*.
3. **do;** *a lot of work to do – viel Arbeit (zu tun)*
4. **do;** *do someone a favour – jmd. einen Gefallen tun*
5. **do;** *do without – verzichten auf, ohne auskommen*
6. **made;** *make a mistake – einen Fehler machen*
7. **do;** *do something again – etwas noch einmal machen*
8. **make;** *make out a cheque – einen Scheck ausstellen*
9. **making;** *make coffee – Kaffee kochen*
10. **did;** *do away with something – abschaffen*
11. **made;** *make a puppet – eine Puppe basteln*
12. **do;** *do with some help – Hilfe (ge)brauchen*

Tipp

Sicher haben Sie festgestellt, dass die englischen Verben *do* und *make* nicht mit *tun* und *machen* im Deutschen gleichzusetzen sind. In einem Wörterbuch können Sie viele weitere Wendungen mit *do* und *make* finden.

6

1. **carrots**
2. **cucumbers**
3. **spinach**
4. **chocolates**. Im Plural einzelne *Pralinen*, im Singular eine Tafel oder ein Riegel Schokolade.
5. **grapes**
6. **tomatoes**. Obwohl sie oft als Gemüse angesehen werden, sind sie eigentlich Früchte.
7. **sausages**. Zu einem traditionellen englischen Frühstück gehören auch (Brat-)Würstchen.
8. **biscuits**. In den USA heißen sie *cookies*.
9. **strawberries**. Werden traditionsgemäß gerne beim Tennis in Wimbledon gegessen.
10. **orange juice**
11. **onions**
12. **grapefruit**
13. **spaghetti**
14. **sandwiches**
15. **ice cream**. Wenn Sie einfach nur *ice* bestellen, bekommen Sie Eiswürfel und kein Speiseeis.

Tipp

Wussten Sie schon, woher das englische *sandwich* seinen Namen hat? Der vierte Earl of Sandwich hatte vor lauter Kartenspielen keine Zeit zum Essen. Darum ließ er sich eine Scheibe Schinken zwischen zwei Brotscheiben legen. So konnte er essen, ohne das Spiel unterbrechen zu müssen.

7

1. **British Broadcasting Company**. Die BBC hat zwei Fernsehkanäle – BBC1 und BBC2 – und diverse Radiostationen. Weltweit kann man z. B. den BBC World Service empfangen.
2. **Automobile Association**. Britischer Automobilklub, wie der ADAC in Deutschland. Die Abkürzung könnte jedoch, je nach Zusammenhang, auch für die Organisation *Anonyme Alkoholiker* (*Alcoholics Anonymous)* stehen.

3. **répondez s'il vous plaît**. Französisch für *Rückantwort erbeten*. Wird häufig auf englischen Einladungen zu Partys verwendet.
4. **Before Christ** und **Anno Domini**. Als Zeitangabe vor Jahreszahlen, z. B. 2000 BC oder 1994 AD.
5. **Central Intelligence Agency**. Bezeichnung für den US-amerikanischen Geheimdienst.
6. **care of**. Etwa: *wohnhaft bei*. Wird bei vorübergehenden Adressen angegeben, z. B. Ms Hilda Bone, c/o Paris Hilton
7. **do it yourself**. *Heimwerken, etwas selber bauen/reparieren*.
8. **Federal Bureau of Investigation**: US-amerikanische Kriminalpolizei.
9. **General Certificate of Secondary Education**. Neue Bezeichnung für Schulabschlussexamen im britischen Schulsystem. Ersetzt den früheren *O level* (mit 16 Jahren) und den *A level* (mit 18 Jahren).
10. **Greenwich Mean Time**. Mittlere Zeit Greenwich oder Greenwicher Zeit, entspricht der WEZ (westeuropäischen Zeit).
11. **I owe you**. Etwa: *Ich schulde dir.* Auf Schuldscheinen.
12. **male chauvenist pig**. Schimpfwort für einen sich Frauen gegenüber chauvinistisch verhaltenden Mann.
13. **Ministry of Transport**. *Verkehrsministerium*. Auch *MOT test,* vergleichbar mit der deutschen TÜV-Prüfung für Automobile.
14. **old age pensioner**. *Rentner/in*.
15. **public relations**. *Werbung/Öffentlichkeitsarbeit*, aber auch die Bezeichnung für die entsprechende Abteilung in einer Firma.
16. **please turn over**. *Bitte umblättern*. Häufig in Briefen am Ende einer Seite.
17. **save our souls**. International anerkanntes Morsezeichen (Notsignal). Über Funk gilt *MAYDAY* (aus dem Französischen *m'aider* für *Hilfe!)*.
18. **unidentified flying object**. *Unbekanntes Flugobjekt*.
19. **value-added tax**. *Mehrwertsteuer.*
20. **very important person**. *Wichtige Person*.
21. **et cetera**. Lateinisch für *usw.*

22. **for example**. Vom Lateinischen *exempli gratia – zum Beispiel.*
23. **that is** oder **that means**. Vom lateinischen *id est – das heißt*.
24. **Bachelor of Arts**. Akademischer Grad, den man nach ca. drei bis vier Jahren Hochschule mit Bestehen der Abschlussprüfung erreicht. Die nächsthöhere Stufe ist *Master of Arts (M.A.)*.
25. **Doctor of Philosophy**. Entspricht dem Doktortitel, wird hinter dem Namen aufgeführt. Achtung: Dieser akademische Grad gilt für alle Studienfächer, nicht nur für Philosophie.

8

1. **unclean** – *unsauber,* auch: *dirty*
2. **ungrateful** – *undankbar*
3. **unfortunately** – *leider*
4. **unfurnished** – *unmöbliert*
5. **inhuman** – *inhuman, unmenschlich*
6. **unemployed** – *arbeitslos*
7. **disappeared** – *verschwunden*
8. **unhurt** – *unverletzt*
9. **uncomfortable** – *unbequem*
10. **impossible** – *unmöglich*
11. **unfair** – *unfair*
12. **unfit** – *unfit, nicht fit*
13. **uncommon** – *selten*
14. **dislike** – *nicht mögen*. Nur bei *like* als Verb gilt die Vorsilbe *dis-*. Wird *like* bei Vergleichen im Sinne von *genauso ... wie* verwendet, lautet das Gegenteil *unlike*.
15. **inexpensive** – *billig, preiswert*
16. **irresponsible** – *unzuverlässig*
17. **unconscious** – *bewusstlos*
18. **disagreement** – *Uneinigkeit*
19. **informal** – *zwanglos*
20. **independent** *(of)* – *unabhängig*

Tipp

Haben Sie die Übung einigermaßen gemeistert? Wenn Sie sich einmal nicht sicher sind, können Sie sich mit dem Wörtchen *not* aus der Klemme helfen, z. B.:

It's inconvenient.	It's not convenient.
That's illegal.	That's not legal.

Die elegantere Lösung bleibt allerdings die erstere.

Eine feste Regel für die Auswahl der richtigen Vorsilbe gibt es leider nicht, aber hier vielleicht eine kleine Hilfe: Die am häufigsten vorkommende Vorsilbe ist *un-*.

9

1. **c)** *New arrival* bezieht sich auf die „Ankunft" des Babys.
2. **g)** Der Wunsch drückt aus, dass die Person noch viele Geburtstage feiern, d. h. noch ein langes Leben vor sich haben möge.
3. **d)** Mit den *little problems* sind *Kinder* gemeint.
4. **j)** Im übertragenen Sinn der Schlüssel zur Tür zum Erwachsensein.
5. **h)**
6. **i)** Zur *Goldenen Hochzeit (golden wedding)*
7. **b)** Eine Tonne wird im Sprachgebrauch für die Zahl 100 gebraucht, z. B. *drive a ton – 100 Meilen/Std. fahren, get a ton* (z. B. beim Cricket) – *100 Punkte erreichen.*
8. **a)** Ein beliebte Redewendung ist: *Life begins at forty.*
9. **f)**
10. **e)** Grüße zur Jahreswende. Üblich sind auch Karten, die *Merry Christmas and a Happy New Year* wünschen. Weihnachtskarten sind in England ein Muss.

Tipp

Glückwünsche werden als Toast ausgesprochen oder sind auf Karten zu finden. Besonders für Geburtstage, aber auch für andere Ereignisse ist die Palette der gesprochenen oder geschriebenen Glückwünsche groß. Kürzere Glückwünsche sind z. B. *Happy birthday!/All the best!/Congratulations!*

Übrigens: Der *Valentinstag (Valentine's Day)* am 14. Februar jedes Jahres ist ein sehr beliebter Tag, um Karten an die/den Liebsten zu senden. Manche Leute setzen auch einen Gruß in die lokale Zeitung. Meistens bleibt der/die Absender/in anonym, was die Sache erst so richtig spannend macht. Ein alter Spruch zum Valentinstag ist:

Roses are red
Violets are blue
Sugar is sweet
And so are you!

10

1. **used to play;** früher *(when we lived in Hamburg)* spielten sie regelmäßig *(regularly)*, heute nicht mehr.
2. **is used to getting up,** d. h. er ist (jetzt) daran gewöhnt, früh aufzustehen.
3. **is used to cutting**
4. **used to play**
5. **is not used to writing**
6. **used to throw**
7. **use to believe;** Achtung: Bei der Verneinung muss als Hilfsverb *did* hinzugenommen werden. Dadurch steht das Verb *use* dann nicht mehr in der Vergangenheitsform (siehe auch Satz 9).
8. **used to swim**
9. **use to think**
10. **is not used to using;** möglich wäre hier auch: *He still is not used to it. – Er hat sich immer noch nicht daran gewöhnt.*

Tipp

Mit *used to* drückt man vergangene Gewohnheiten aus, also etwas, was man früher regelmäßig gemacht hat, z. B.: *In England he used to get up at 8 o'clock in the morning* (früher). Meistens kann man anhand einer Zeitangabe erkennen, ob es sich um eine frühere Gewohnheit handelt, z. B. *when David was young/between 1984 and 1989/until.*

Wenn man etwas (zur Zeit) gewöhnt ist, so verwendet man *to be used to*, wobei das nachfolgende Verb immer mit *-ing* gebildet wird, z. B.: *When he came to Germany he found it very hard to get up so early in the morning. Now he is used to getting up at 6.30 each morning.* – Jetzt hat er sich daran gewöhnt.

11

1. **arm**
2. **elbow**; der Nerv, der so kitzelt, wenn man sich den Ellbogen an einer Kante anschlägt, heißt *funny bone (Mäuschen, Musikantenknochen)*.
3. **head**
4. **eye**
5. **nose**; *nosey – neugierig.*
6. **mouth**
7. **ear**
8. **neck**; *throat – Hals.*
9. **wrist**
10. **hand**
11. **fingers**
12. **thumb**
13. **shoulder**
14. **waist**
15. **stomach**; Kinder nennen den *Bauch* häufig *tummy*. Umgangssprachlich heißt er auch *belly*; daher stammen auch die folgenden Wörter: *belly button – Bauchnabel, belly dancing – Bauchtanz, beer belly – Bierbauch, to belly ache – quengeln.*
16. **knee**
17. **leg**
18. **foot**
19. **ankle**
20. **toes**

Tipp

Für die diversen Schmerzen gibt es im Englischen verschiedene Wörter:

- *Ache*, z. B. *backache, toothache, headache, stomach-ache*. Hier lässt sich der Schmerz nicht genau lokalisieren. *Ache* kann auch als Verb verwendet werden, z. B. *My legs ache. – Meine Beine tun mir weh.*
- *Pain* bezieht sich auf einen genau lokalisierbaren, scharfen Schmerz, kann aber auch im übertragenen Sinne verwendet werden, z. B. *He is a pain in the neck. – Er nervt.*
- *Sore,* Eigenschaftswort, z. B. bei Halsschmerzen *(sore throat)*. Kinder verwenden oft das Wort *sore,* wenn sie mitteilen wollen, dass ihnen etwas weh tut, z. B. *I have a sore arm*. Achtung: *Sore* bedeutet in den USA *auch ärgerlich*.

12

1. **carefully**, bezieht sich auf *drives;* **slowly**, bezieht sich auf *was driving;* **quick**, bezieht sich auf *reactions;* **quickly,** bezieht sich auf *managed to stop;* **seriously**, bezieht sich auf *hurt*.
2. **carefully**, bezieht sich auf *does (her work);* **excellent**, bezieht sich auf *dancer;* **fluently**, bezieht sich auf *can speak;* **good**, bezieht sich auf *cook;* **good**, bezieht sich auf *tasted*.
3. **expensive**, bezieht sich auf *house;* **cheaply**, bezieht sich auf *bought;* **quickly**, bezieht sich auf *delivered;* **heavy**, bezieht sich auf *things;* **heavily**, bezieht sich auf *fell;* **badly**, bezieht sich auf *damaged*.

Tipp

Ein Adverb bezieht sich in der Regel auf ein Verb, z. B.: *He drives carefully*. Es kann aber auch ein anderes Adjektiv beschreiben, z. B. *seriously ill – ernstlich krank*. Die meisten Adverben erkennt man an der Endung „*-ly*". Es gibt natürlich auch Ausnahmen, z. B. *good – well; fast – fast*.

Das Adjektiv beschreibt in der Regel ein Substantiv, das meistens nach dem Adjektiv steht, z. B. *the careful driver, a good friend, the slow worker*. Vorsicht: Einige Verben werden grundsätzlich mit einem Adjektiv beschrieben, z. B. *she looks good/it sounds good/he feels good/it tastes good/it smells good*.

Eine ältere Guinness-Werbung lautete:
"It looks good, it tastes good and by golly *(Menschenskind)* it does you good!"

13

1. **gang** (auch: **mob**) – *Gang* oder *Bande*. Das Wort *mob* wird eher im Zusammenhang mit großen Städten verwendet.
2. **tomboy** – *Wildfang*. Das Wort setzt sich zusammen aus *tom (Kater)* und *boy (Junge)*.
3. **rough** – *grob*
4. **orchard** – *Obstgarten*
5. **turf** – *Boden, Torf,* hier etwa *Revier*
6. **scrumping** – *Äpfel stehlen*. Der englische *Apfelwein (cider)* wird auch *scrumpy* genannt und ist in Südwestengland sehr beliebt.
7. **conker** – *(Ross)Kastanie*

Tipp

Im Text kommen zwei Kinderspiele vor, von denen Sie eines bestimmt auch kennen: *hide-and-seek – Versteckspiel*.
Ein weiteres beliebtes Spiel, *conkers,* für das man Kastanien braucht, geht folgendermaßen: Eine Kastanie wird an ein Band gebunden und gegen die Kastanie eines anderen Kindes geschlagen. Gewonnen hat das Kind, dessen Kastanie am längsten hält.

Kennen Sie die folgenden Wörter, die auch im Text vorkommen?

horse chestnut	Rosskastanie
initiation ceremony	Aufnahmeprüfung, Initiation
kid	umgangssprachlich für Kind
recruit	Anfänger, Neuling
savvy	schlau, geschickt
vouch	sich für jemanden verbürgen

14

1. **out;** *take someone out – jemanden einladen, mit jemandem ausgehen*
2. **up;** *take up – anfangen*
3. **off;** *take something off – etwas ausziehen*
4. **over;** *get over something – über etwas hinwegkommen*
5. **by;** *get by – zurechtkommen*
6. **up;** *get up – aufstehen*
7. **out;** *try out – ausprobieren*
8. **on;** *try it on* – hier: *sehen, wie weit man gehen kann*
9. **for;** *try for – suchen*
10. **out of;** *run out of – ausgehen, zu Ende gehen*
11. **into;** *run into someone – jemanden zufällig treffen*
12. **after;** *run after someone – jemandem hinterherlaufen*

Tipp

Ein Verb, das zusammen mit einer Präposition eine andere Bedeutung erhält, nennt man im Englischen *phrasal verb*. *Phrasal verbs* werden besonders in der gesprochenen oder Umgangssprache verwendet.

Mit Hilfe von Karteikarten können Sie diese Wörter leichter lernen. Schreiben Sie den englischen Begriff auf die eine, die deutsche Bedeutung und einen Beispielsatz auf die andere Seite und fragen Sie sich mit Hilfe der Kärtchen regelmäßig ab.

→ Zum Thema „Präpositionen“ siehe Übung 16.

15

1. **a)** George Washington (1732 – 1799) war der erste Präsident der Vereinigten Staaten. Sein Geburtstag, der 22. Februar, ist ein nationaler Feiertag.
2. **c)** John Brown (1800 – 1859) war ein überzeugter Gegner der Sklaverei in den Vereinigten Staaten. Er wurde wegen Verrats gehängt, nachdem er bei einem Überfall auf ein Waffenlager zur Vorbereitung eines Sklavenaufstandes festgenommen worden war.
3. **a)** Der Weihnachtsmann heißt *Father Christmas* oder *Santa Claus* (USA).
4. **c)** Sir Walter Raleigh (1552 – 1618) wurde nach einer erfolglosen Südamerikaexpedition von James I. zum Tod durch das Schafott verurteilt.
5. **b)** Florence Nightingale (1820 – 1910) arbeitete u. a. von 1853 bis 1856 als Krankenschwester während des Krimkrieges.
6. **c)** Abraham Lincoln (1809 – 1865) war der 16. Präsident der Vereinigten Staaten und setzte sich aktiv für die Abschaffung der Sklaverei ein. Er wurde während eines Theaterbesuchs von dem Schauspieler John Wilkes Booth erschossen.
7. **c)** Andere berühmt gewordene Figuren aus den „Peanuts“ sind Woodstock, Lucy, Linus, Schröder und Peppermint Patty.
8. **b)** Auf einem kleinen Zettel steht in ein oder zwei Sätzen, was die Zukunft für diese Person bringen wird. *Fortune* heißt zwar auch Vermögen, hier jedoch bedeutet es soviel wie *Schicksal*. Ein *fortune-teller* ist ein/e Wahrsager/in.

➜ Weitere landeskundliche Informationen finden Sie in den Übungen 18 und 26.

16

Lösungswort: **ABRACADABRA**

1. **at;** normalerweise arbeitet man bei *(at)* einer Firma. Dagegen sagt man häufig *for*, wenn man z. B. in freier Mitarbeit für ein Unternehmen tätig ist *(freelancer – freie/r Mitarbeiter/in)*. Sagt jemand *I work with Dodds & Co*, so handelt es sich um eine Kooperation, bei der der/die Sprecher/in evtl. eine eigene Firma hat.
2. **in**; bei Abteilungen.
3. **next to**
4. **at**; immer bei *at the end/at the beginning of*. Steht nur der Monat oder das Jahr, dann heißt es *in*, z. B. *in January/in 1849*. Der generelle Beginn oder das Ende einer Sache wird auch mit *in* formuliert, z. B. *In the beginning (anfangs) I didn't like my job* oder *Everything worked out alright in the end (schließlich)*.
5. **on**; bei Wochentagen.
6. **at**; *at* bedeutet hier *im* Kino. *At the cinema* kann aber auch *vor dem Kino* bedeuten, wenn man einen Treffpunkt ausmacht.
7. **by**; gilt für alle Verkehrsmittel. Aber: *zu Fuß – on foot*.
8. **at**; bei Uhrzeiten.
9. **in**; Auto fahren allgemein heißt zwar *go by car, mit einem Auto* oder *in einem Auto (mit)fahren* heißt jedoch *go in a car*.
10. **next to**
11. **at**

Tipp

Sie haben sicher schon festgestellt, dass sich die Präpositionen meistens nicht ins Englische übersetzen lassen. Deshalb hier einige Hilfen zu den verschiedenen Zeitangaben:

on: bei Wochentagen und allen Feiertagen, in denen das Wort *day* vorkommt, z. B. *on Christmas Day*.
at: bei Uhrzeiten und Feiertagen, z. B. *at Christmas*.
in: bei Monaten, Jahren und Jahreszeiten. Achtung: Bei Jahreszahlen steht im Englischen immer die Präposition *in*.

17

1. **beach** *(Strand); beech – Buche*
2. **cellar** *(Keller); seller – Verkäufer/in.* Achtung: Nicht verwechseln mit *der Verkäuferin/dem Verkäufer in einem Geschäft (shop assistant).*
3. **heard** *(hear – hören); herd – Herde*
4. **blew** *(blow – blasen); blue – blau*
5. **bored** *(gelangweilt); board – Brett*
6. **buoy** *(Boje); boy – Junge*
7. **brake** *(Bremse); break – brechen, kaputtmachen*
8. **here** *(hier); hear – hören*
9. **fair** *(fair, gerecht); fare – Fahrgeld*
10. **hire** *(Vermietung, Ausleihe); higher – höher*
11. **hair** *(Haar); hare – Hase*
12. **hart** *(Hirsch); heart – Herz*
13. **whole** *(ganz); hole – Loch, Grube*
14. **key** *(Schlüssel); quay – Kai*
15. **meet** *(treffen); meat – Fleisch*
16. **knows** *(know – kennen); nose – Nase*
17. **pears** *(Birnen); pairs – Paare*
18. **peace** *(Frieden); piece – Teil, Stück*
19. **rows** *(Reihen); rose – Rose.* Aber auch Vergangenheit von *rise (steigen, sich erheben).*
20. **profit** *(Profit, Gewinn); prophet – Prophet*

Tipp

Im Englischen gibt es viele gleichlautende (homophone) Wörter, die unterschiedlich geschrieben werden und auch verschiedene Bedeutungen haben. Welches Wort gemeint ist, können Sie beim Hören nur aus dem Zusammenhang erschließen.

18

1. **Falsch**. *Guy Fawkes Night* ist ein britisches Fest zur Erinnerung an den gerade noch verhinderten Sprengstoffanschlag auf das Parlament am 5. November 1605. Am Abend werden Feuer entzündet und ein Feuerwerk veranstaltet. Dieser Tag ist allerdings kein öffentlicher Feiertag.

2. **Falsch**. Die Geschenke werden am Morgen des 25. Dezember geöffnet.
3. **Falsch**. Der 4. Juli ist ein nationaler Feiertag, und zwar der Unabhängigkeitstag. An diesem Tag wird das Inkrafttreten der amerikanischen Unabhängigkeitserklärung gefeiert.
4. **Richtig**. Halloween *(Hallowed Evening – heiliger Vorabend)* ist die Nacht vor Allerheiligen. An diesem Abend werden allerlei Späße gemacht, und man verkleidet sich. Ein Brauch besteht darin, dass Kinder von Haus zu Haus gehen und mit den Worten *„Trick or Treat"* um Gaben bitten. Gibt man ihnen nichts, so spielen sie einem einen Streich.
5. **Richtig**. Das erste Erntedankfest wurde zusammen mit den Indianern gefeiert, die den Siedlern den Anbau von Mais gezeigt hatten. *Thanksgiving Day* wird in den USA an jedem vierten Donnerstag im November (in Kanada an jedem zweiten Montag im Oktober) gefeiert und gilt als einer der wichtigsten Feiertage in den Vereinigten Staaten.
6. **Falsch**. Wenn ein Feiertag wie der 25. oder 26. Dezember auf ein Wochenende fällt, wird der darauffolgende Montag zum Feiertag. Als 1994 beide Feiertage auf ein Wochenende fielen, wurden sogar der darauffolgende Montag und Dienstag zu freien Tagen.
7. **Falsch**. So heißt dieser Tag nur in Deutschland.
8. **Richtig**. Der Geburtstag der Königin ist eigentlich der 21. April. Die offizielle Geburtstagsparade findet jedoch immer am zweiten Samstag im Juni statt. Keiner der Tage ist ein öffentlicher Feiertag.
9. **Richtig**. An diesem Tag gingen Lehrlinge und andere Angestellte mit einem Karton *(box)* bei den Kunden ihrer Arbeitgeber herum, um kleine Geschenke zu sammeln. Noch heute ist es üblich, den Postboten oder dem Zeitungsjungen zu Weihnachten eine Kleinigkeit zu schenken *(Christmas box)*.
10. **Richtig**.
11. **Richtig**. Der erste Montag im Mai (nach dem 1. Mai) und der letzte Montag im August. *Bank holidays* werden in Großbritannien Feiertage genannt, an denen Banken und auch die meisten Geschäfte geschlossen haben.

12. **Richtig**. Das Wort kommt von *White Sunday*. *Pfingsten* wird auch *Pentecost* genannt.
13. **Falsch**. St. David ist der Schutzpatron von Wales. Der Schutzpatron von Schottland ist St. Andrew, von England ist es St. George.
14. **Richtig**. St. Patrick ist der Schutzpatron von Irland. Da es in den USA viele irische Einwanderer gibt, wird auch dort am 17. März mit Paraden gefeiert.
15. **Richtig**. Der Abend des 25. Januar ist Robert Burns, einem der bekanntesten schottischen Dichter, gewidmet.

19

	5.								
1.	T	i	n	a					
2.	A	l	f	r	e	d			
3.	K	i	n	g					
4.	E	l	i	z	a	b	e	t	h

5.								
T	u	r	n	e	r			
H	i	t	c	h	c	o	c	k
A	r	t	h	u	r			
T	a	y	l	o	r			

Lösung: **TAKE THAT**

Tipp

Die Legende besagt, dass King Arthur um das Jahr 500 bis 600 n. Chr. gelebt habe. Nicht nur in Cornwall, auch in Wales, Cumberland, Schottland und sogar in der französischen Bretagne beansprucht man ihn als Nationalhelden. In Cornwall meint man, er habe in der Burg von Tintagel gelebt. Noch heute warten viele auf die Rückkehr von King Arthur.

20

1. **repeat**
2. **you**
3. **tell**
4. **information**
5. **about**
6. **learning**
7. **name**
8. **travel**
9. **reserve**
10. **spell**

Lösungswort: **POLITENESS**

Tipp

Im Englischen sollten Sie nicht mit *please* und *excuse me* sparen! Nach Fragen oder Bitten um etwas macht es sich immer gut, wenn man noch ein *please* anhängt. Achtung: Niemals mit *please* antworten, wenn sich jemand bei Ihnen bedankt, sondern z. B. *You're welcome* oder *Not at all* sagen. Wenn Sie aber beim Essen etwas weiterreichen und jemand bedankt sich, so brauchen Sie darauf nicht zu antworten.

Wenn Sie eine fremde Person auf der Straße etwas fragen möchten, beginnen Sie am besten immer mit *Excuse me.* Wenn Sie irgendwo im Gedränge durchgelassen werden möchten, sagen Sie auch: *Excuse me?,* was etwa so viel bedeutet wie *Darf ich bitte mal durch*?

Wenn Sie sich im Geschäft für etwas entschieden haben, sagen Sie z. B. *I'll take this dress*. Ohne *will ('ll)* klingt der Satz unhöflich.

21

1. **is committed**. *Sich engagieren* kann auch *be involved* sein, aber nicht: *engaged – verlobt*.
2. **donated**. Bei Geld-, aber auch bei Blutspenden. Aber nicht: *spend* – (Geld) *ausgeben,* (Zeit) *verbringen*.
3. **ticket**. Für alle Eintrittskarten, Fahrkarten usw. Aber nicht: *card*, z. B. *birthday card*. Die *Speisekarte* heißt *menu*.
4. **make**. Aber nicht: *cook*. Das heißt zwar *kochen*, bezieht sich aber eher allgemein auf das Zubereiten von Speisen. Bei Wasser heißt es *boil*.
5. **check**. Aber nicht: *control – steuern, regulieren*.
6. **vintage cars**. Aber nicht: *oldtimer*. Im Englischen bedeutet *old-timer* so viel wie *alter Hase*.
7. **borrow**. Aber nicht: *lend*. Das heißt zwar auch *(aus)leihen*, aber im Sinne von *geben. Can I borrow some money from you?* Aber: *Can you lend me some money?*

8. **What do you think?** oder **What's your opinion?** Aber nicht: *mean – bedeuten*.
9. **do not have/need to go**. Aber nicht: *must not* – meist: *nicht brauchen/dürfen*.
10. **wants**. Aber nicht: *will – werden*. Mit dem Hilfsverb *will* wird die Zukunft gebildet, z. B. *I will buy some ice cream tomorrow*. Es kann nicht als selbständiges Verb alleine stehen. *Wollen* ist *want* oder *would like*.

Tipp

„Falsche Freunde" sind Wörter, die sich im Englischen und im Deutschen von ihrer Schreibweise her sehr ähneln, aber von ihrer Bedeutung her verschieden sind. Also Vorsicht, wenn ein Wort „zu einfach" aussieht. Es könnte ein „falscher Freund" sein.

➜ Weitere „falsche Freunde" finden Sie in Übung 31.

22

1. **right**; sagt man auch, wenn man etwas verstanden hat.
2. **book**; *you've been booked* sagt man auch, wenn man einen Strafzettel für falsches Parken erhält.
3. **cold**; übrigens: In England *fängt* man eine Erkältung *(catch a cold)*.
4. **cross**; auch *ärgerlich,* heißt im britischen Englisch *cross*, in den USA sagt man *mad*.
5. **drop**
6. **express**
7. **face**; *face up to the truth* heißt *der Wahrheit ins Gesicht sehen*, *lose face* bedeutet *das Gesicht verlieren*.
8. **fair**; auch im Deutschen spricht man von *Fair Play*. Geht es nicht fair zu, sagt man auch *It's not cricket!*
9. **fine**; als Substantiv im Sinne von *Strafe*, aber auch als Verb, z. B. *I got fined for speeding*.
10. **fire**; umgangssprachlich für *entlassen*, sonst: *dismiss*.
11. **block**; in Großbritannien *block of flats*.
12. **kind**
13. **last**
14. **lift**, (give a ~) auch: *Fahrstuhl*, in den USA *elevator*.

15. **change**
16. **play**
17. **press**
18. **record**; auch: *Schallplatte*.
19. **second**
20. **sentence**
21. **square**
22. **slip**
23. **stamp**; kann auch *stempeln* heißen.
24. **yard**; eine Meile entspricht 1760 Yards bzw. 1,6 km. In den USA bedeutet das Wort *yard Garten* oder *Hof* hinter dem Haus.

Tipp

Sicher ist Ihnen aufgefallen, dass viele Wörter sowohl Verb als auch Substantiv sein können, z. B.:

fine	eine Geldstrafe geben, Geldstrafe
lift	anheben, Fahrstuhl
change	ändern, Änderung, Kleingeld
sentence	verurteilen, Urteil/Strafe

Diese Art von Rätsel ist sehr beliebt und kommt auch in englischen Zeitungen häufig vor. Meistens befindet es sich in der farbigen Sonderbeilage, die der Wochenendausgabe der Zeitung beiliegt *(Sunday supplement)*. Vielleicht finden Sie einige Wörter, mit denen Sie Ihr eigenes Rätsel erstellen können?

23

1. **Beide sind möglich**. *When* ist aber besser, da man davon ausgeht, dass die Bedienung irgendwann kommt. *If* wäre für den Fall richtig, dass man schon lange wartet und davon ausgeht, dass die Bedienung schon Feierabend gemacht hat.
2. **If**
3. **When**
4. **If**
5. **If**

6. **When**. Wenn jemand Ihnen *It is my treat* sagt, bedeutet es, dass Sie eingeladen sind. Es ist eher informell und wird bei kleineren Einladungen (z. B. Kaffee, Eis) verwendet.
7. **When**
8. **If**
9. **If**
10. **If**
11. **Beide sind möglich**. *If*, wenn Sie glauben, dass man Sie vergessen hat; *when*, wenn Sie damit rechnen, dass das Essen noch kommt.
12. **When**
13. **If**
14. **If**
15. **When**

Tipp

Aufgepasst, für die deutsche Konjunktion *wenn* gibt es im Englischen zwei Wörter:

- *when:* nur zeitlich im Sinne von *sobald*
- *if:* meistens: *für den Fall, dass ...*

Die Bedingungssätze können, müssen aber nicht mit einem Komma getrennt werden, z. B. *When the waiter comes, I will order the fish.*
Sie können den Satz übrigens auch umkehren und die Bedingung ans Ende stellen, z. B. *I will order fish when the waiter comes.* In diesem Fall darf vor dem *if/when* kein Komma stehen!

Übrigens: *Worcester(sauce)* in Satz 12 wird „wuster“ ausgesprochen.

24

1. **Yes**. Vorausgesetzt, das Fahrzeug wird bis zum 15. März abgeholt, weil *commencing between 15 Jan and 15 March*.
2. **£76**. Preis pro Woche, weil *all weekly rates*.
3. **(416) 673-6690**.
4. **Nothing**. Der Ausdruck *call collect* bedeutet, dass die Person, die angerufen wurde, das Gespräch bezahlt. In Großbritannien heißt das *reverse charge*.
5. **Peugot 505**, er wird als *Family Estate* bezeichnet.
6. **Yes**. Die Versicherung läuft über den Automobilclub AA *(Automobile Association)* und deckt Pannenhilfe *(Full AA breakdown cover)*.
7. **Yes**. *VAT* (*value added tax*) ist die *Mehrwertsteuer*. *All rates plus VAT 17.5%*.
8. **Nothing**. *Free delivery and collection on all rentals*.
9. **Yes**. Siehe letzte Zeile: *24 hours*.
10. **Austin Montego** (*2.0HL* und *1.6L)* und **Ford Granada** (*2.8i Ghia* und *2.0i)*.

Tipp

Möglicherweise wird man Sie fragen, ob Sie *CDW* (*Collision Damage Waiver*) wünschen. Das spart Ihnen die Selbstbeteiligung an möglichen Kosten, auch wenn Sie einen Unfall schuldhaft verursachen.

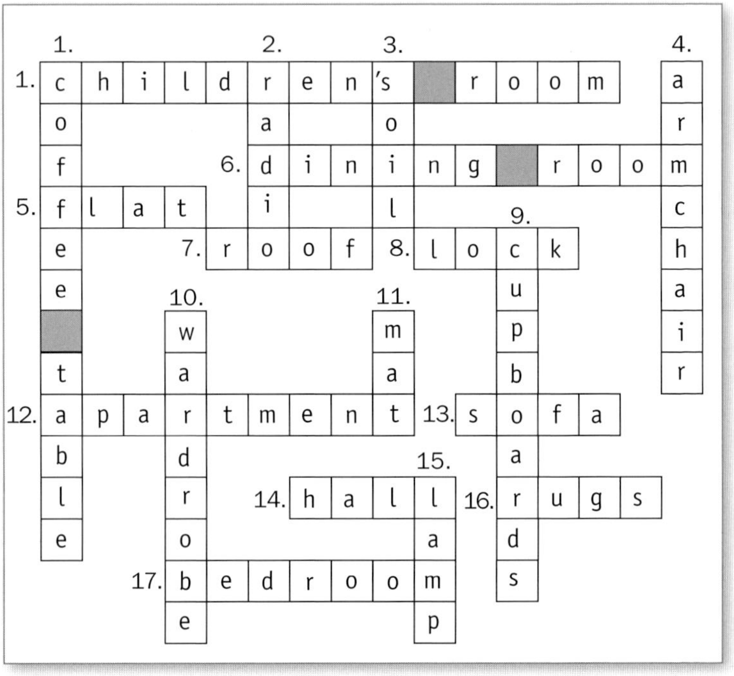

Tipp

Hier einige weitere wichtige Räume:

Küche	kitchen
Wohnzimmer	living room, lounge
Bad	bathroom
Keller	cellar
Dachboden	attic
Arbeitszimmer	study

26

1. **Richtig.** Nicht zu verwechseln mit dem deutschen Wort *Pantomime*. In Großbritannien wird ein *pantomime* traditionell zu Weihnachten aufgeführt.
2. **Richtig.** Typische Hochzeitsutensilien sind z. B. ein Strumpfband, das später den männlichen Gästen zugeworfen wird, und ein Brautstrauß für die weiblichen Gäste. Wer den Gegenstand auffängt, so sagt man, wird als Nächstes heiraten.
3. **Richtig.** Nach der Überlieferung trat im Kampf zwischen England und Schottland ein schottischer Soldat auf eine Distel. Der Schrei, den er daraufhin ausstieß, weckte den Kampfgeist der anderen schottischen Soldaten und sie besiegten daraufhin die Engländer.
4. **Falsch.** Die Freiheitsstatue steht auf Liberty Island/ New York.
5. **Richtig.** Das Lied heißt „Auld Lang Syne".
6. **Richtig.**
7. **Richtig.** *Take-away* bedeutet hier *Gericht zum Mitnehmen*. Man kann nicht nur „Fish & Chips", sondern auch indische und chinesische Gerichte zum Mitnehmen kaufen.
8. **Richtig.** *Crisps* sind *Kartoffelchips*. Aber Vorsicht: In den USA heißen die Kartoffelchips *potato chips*. In Großbritannien wiederum sagt man zu *Pommes frites* *chips* (siehe *fish and chips*).
9. **Richtig.** Früher (vor 1960) war dies eine Silbermünze, z. B. ein alter *sixpence*.

Tipp

Wussten Sie, dass das Gebäude in dem Bild auf Seite 57 *St. Stephen's Tower* ist? Nur die darin befindliche Glocke heißt *Big Ben*.

→ Weitere landeskundliche Informationen finden Sie in den Übungen 15 und 18.

27

1. **g)** *Unterhemd*. Achtung: Im amerikanischen Englisch bedeutet *vest Weste* (siehe Nr. 5).
2. **i)** Aufgepasst: Im britischen Englisch bedeutet *pants Herrenunterwäsche*.
3. **h)** Manche sagen auch *bathrobe* und alle drei Begriffe werden in beiden Ländern verwendet.
4. **a)** *Pumps/plimsoles* waren in der Regel aus Stoff und hatten eine Gummisohle. Heute werden *Turnschuhe* sowohl in den USA als auch in England eher als *trainers* bezeichnet.
5. **j)** *Weste* (siehe Nr. 1).
6. **l)** In Großbritannien wurden die Gummistiefel nach dem Duke of Wellington benannt, der diese Schuhe getragen hat. Meistens wird die Abkürzung *Wellies* verwendet.
7. **k)** *Damenstrumpfhose;* sowohl in Großbritannien als auch in den USA wird *tights* verwendet.
8. **f)** *Nylonstrümpfe*
9. **c)** Sowohl in Großbritannien als auch in den USA wird das Wort *pullover* verwendet. Die Kurzform *Pulli* wie im Deutschen gibt es jedoch nicht.
10. **d)** Achtung: *purse* wird im britischen Englisch für *Portmonee* verwendet.
11. **b)** Im britischen Englisch wird *wallet* eher für *(Herren-)Brieftasche* verwendet, während das *(Damen-)Portmonee* dort *purse* heißt.
12. **e)** Der *Regenmantel* wurde in Großbritannien nach Charles Macintosh (1766 – 1843) benannt, einem schottischen Chemiker, der 1823 wasserdichtes Material patentiert hat.

Tipp

Die Unterschiede zwischen britischem und amerikanischem Englisch verschwimmen heutzutage immer mehr. Viele amerikanische Ausdrücke sind auch in Großbritannien gebräuchlich (eher als umgekehrt).
Bei Wörtern, die auf beiden Seiten des Atlantiks vorkommen, wie z. B. *purse* oder *vest*, kann man immer noch aus dem Zusammenhang erschließen, welche Bedeutung gemeint ist.

Es ist interessant, dass einige der amerikanischen Wörter direkte Übersetzungen aus dem Deutschen sind. Die Ausnahme ist *Pullover*; hier wurde das deutsche Wort aus dem Englischen übernommen: *pull over – überziehen.*

28

1. **will**
2. **would**
3. **will**; *unless* bedeutet hier: Wenn der Kellner nicht bald kommt, ...
4. **will**
5. **would**
6. **will not** (Kurzform: **won't**); *unless*: Wenn es keinen italienischen Wein gibt, ...
7. **would**
8. **would**
9. **will not** (Kurzform: **won't**); *unless*: Wenn du nicht das ganze Gemüse aufisst, ...
10. **will**; *as long as:* Wenn alle einverstanden sind ...
11. **will**; *provided:* Vorausgesetzt, ihr seid alle einverstanden ...

Tipp

Als Faustregel gilt:

- Hält man etwas für sehr wahrscheinlich, so verwendet man im if-Satz die Gegenwart gefolgt von *will*, z. B. *If the strawberries are fresh, I will eat some.* Hier rechnet man stark damit, dass die Erdbeeren frisch sind.
- Hält man etwas für weniger wahrscheinlich oder gar unwahrscheinlich, wählt man im if-Satz die Vergangenheit, gefolgt von *would*, z. B. *If the strawberries were fresh, I would eat some*. Es wird damit gerechnet, dass sie nicht frisch sind.

Beide Bedingungssätze beziehen sich auf die Zukunft. Auf die Vergangenheit bezieht sich nur die folgende Aussage: *If the strawberries had been fresh, I would have eaten them.* Diese Situation ist abgeschlossen. Die Erdbeeren waren nicht frisch, so dass sie nicht gegessen wurden.

29

1. **office block**, in allen anderen wohnt man.
2. **chair**, alle drei anderen Wörter bedeuten *Sofa*.
3. **paintbrush**, zum Malen, alle anderen zum Schreiben. *Biro* war in GB ursprünglich ein Markenname, der jetzt oft generell für Kugelschreiber verwendet wird.
4. **car**, da nur mit dem PKW Personen transportiert werden.
5. **tent**, alle anderen sind feste Gebäude.
6. **film**, als Einziges bewegliche Bilder.
7. **chicken**, die anderen drei sind Haustiere.
8. **elephant**, alle anderen sind Kurzformen *(crocodile, hippopotamus* und *rhinoceros)*.
9. **orange**, da Obst und kein Gemüse.
10. **pump**, muss nicht an einem verkehrstüchtigen Fahrrad vorhanden sein.
11. **bottle opener**, da kein Essbesteck.
12. **path**, *(Spazier)Weg* nur für Fußgänger, z. B. *public footpath*.
13. **Morgan**, die einzige englische Automarke.
14. **green**, alle anderen sind Primärfarben, nur Grün ist eine Mischung aus Gelb und Blau.
15. **cassette**, alle anderen sind Zubehör für Computer.

Tipp

Ein *semidetached house* ist eine *Doppelhaushälfte*, ein *Einzelhaus* ist ein *detached house*. Ein *Reihenhaus* nennt man in England *terraced house (row house* in den USA). Alle vier Begriffe bezeichnen *Gebäude (buildings)*. Unter einem *Haus (house)* versteht man im Englischen nur ein *Wohnhaus*. Eine *Wohnung* wird in Großbritannien als *flat* bezeichnet, in den USA als *apartment*.

Die *Autobahn* heißt in Großbritannien *motorway* und in den USA *freeway*. Das Wort *way* allein kann nicht mit *Straße/Weg* übersetzt werden. Man benutzt *way* z. B., wenn man einen Weg beschreibt: *This is the way to Oxford*.

30

1. **called**
2. **had**
3. **felt**
4. **turned**
5. **dressed**
6. **said**
7. **dropped**
8. **ran**
9. **explained**
10. **met**
11. **wanted**
12. **gave**
13. **decided**
14. **went**
15. **found**
16. **answered**
17. **demanded**
18. **did**
19. **surprised**

Moral: *You can never run away from your fate!*

Tipp

Gute Nachrichten zum Thema „Verben": Die Verbformen im Englischen sind relativ übersichtlich. Neben der Grundform *(call)* gibt es die einfache Vergangenheit *(called)* und das Partizip Perfekt *(called)*. Die letzteren sind bei den regelmäßigen und einigen unregelmäßigen Verben sogar identisch. Hier die Formen zu den unregelmäßigen Verben im Text:

go	went	gone
run	ran	run
meet	met	met
do	did	done
find	found	found
give	gave	given
feel	felt	felt
have	had	had
say	said	said

Und noch eine gute Nachricht: Außer in der Gegenwart *(present simple)* bleiben die Verben in jeder Person unverändert, z. B. *I/you/he/she/it/we/you/they said*.

31

1. become – **werden**
   bekommen – **get, obtain, receive**
2. card – **Grußkarte, Pappe**
   Karte – **menu** *(Speisekarte)*, aber auch: **ticket** *(Kino-/Theaterkarte, Fahrkarte)*
3. chef – **Koch/Köchin**
   Chef – **boss** oder manchmal **superior** *(Vorgesetzte/r)*
4. concern – **betreffen**
   Konzern – **company, firm** (selten *concern*)
5. gift – **Geschenk**
   Gift – **poison**
6. map – **Landkarte**
   Mappe – **case, folder**
7. menu – **Speisekarte**
   Menü – **set meal, special**
8. prospect(s) – **Aussicht(en)**
   Prospekt – **leaflet, pamphlet, brochure**

9. receipt – **Quittung**
   Rezept – **prescription** (vom Arzt), aber auch: **recipe** *(Koch-/Backrezept)*
10. stream – **Bach**
   Strom – **current** (sowohl der *elektrische Strom* als auch die *Strömung* in einem Fluss oder im Meer)
11. eventually – **schließlich**
   eventuell – **possibly**
12. gymnasium – **Sporthalle**
   Gymnasium – **grammar school**
13. pension – **Rente**
   Pension – **guest house, boarding house**
14. sensible – **vernünftig**
   sensibel – **sensitive**
15. warehouse – **Lager(halle)**
   Warenhaus – **department store**

Tipp

Für ein Wort gibt es je nach Kontext immer mehrere Übersetzungen, die hier nicht alle aufgeführt werden können. Wenn Sie über ein Wort mehr wissen möchten, dann schlagen Sie am besten in einem Wörterbuch nach.

➜ Weitere „falsche Freunde“ finden Sie in Übung 21.

32

1. **boot** – *Kofferraum*
2. **windscreen** – *Windschutzscheibe*
3. **windscreen wiper** – *Scheibenwischer*
4. **bonnet** – *Motorhaube*
5. **exhaust pipe** – *Auspuff*
6. **tyre** – *Reifen*
7. **indicator light** – *Blinker*
8. **headlight** – *Scheinwerfer*
9. **number plate** (also licence plate) – *Nummernschild*
10. **bumper** – *Stoßstange*
11. **rear-view mirror** – *Rückspiegel*
12. **horn** – *Hupe*
13. **steering wheel** – *Lenkrad*
14. **indicator** – *Blinkhebel*

15. **ignition** – *Zündung*
16. **hand brake** – *Handbremse*
17. **gear lever** – *Gangschaltung*
18. **clutch** – *Kupplungspedal*
19. **brake** – *Bremspedal*
20. **accelerator** – *Gaspedal*

Tipp

In Sachen Kfz und Autofahren gibt es zwischen britischem und amerikanischem Englisch einige Unterschiede:

GB	**USA**	
accelerator	*auch* gas pedal	Gaspedal
bonnet	hood	Motorhaube
boot	trunk	Kofferraum
flat tyre/puncture	flat	Plattfuß
indicator light	turn signal, blinker	Blinker
lorry	truck	LKW
motorway	freeway	Autobahn
pavement	sidewalk	Fußweg
petrol	gas	Benzin
toll road	turnpike	Straße mit Mautgebühr
windscreen	windshield	Windschutzscheibe

In den USA gibt es noch die Straßenbezeichnungen *highway (Schnellstraße)* und *interstate* (Straße, die zwei Bundesstaaten miteinander verbindet).

33

1. **work**, weil Beruf.
2. **plays**, weil regelmäßig *(every Friday evening)*.
3. **read**, weil mehr oder weniger regelmäßig.
4. **leaves**, weil Fahrplan.
5. **starts**, weil feste Anfangs- und Endzeit.
6. **am playing**, weil *at the moment*.
7. **is trying**, weil gerade in diesem Moment.
8. **live**, weil dauerhaft.
9. **is leaving**, Achtung: weil geplantes Ereignis in der Zukunft.
10. **lasts**; *is lasting* wäre sehr ungewöhnlich.
11. **am doing**, weil gerade in diesem Moment.
12. **writes**, weil regelmäßig *(all her letters)*.
13. **travels**, weil regelmäßig *(once a month)*.
14. **takes**, weil dauerhafter Zustand.
15. **are shopping**, weil *now*.

Tipp

Allgemeine Aussagen werden in der einfachen Gegenwart *(present simple)* ausgedrückt. Dazu gehört alles Regelmäßige bzw. alles, was über einen unbestimmten Zeitraum hinaus gilt, z. B. Aussagen über den Beruf, Fahrpläne usw. „Signalwörter" sind z. B. *every Friday, usually*.
Wenn man jedoch auf etwas aufmerksam machen möchte, weil es gerade abläuft, so wird die Verlaufsform *(present continuous)* verwendet. Achten Sie auch hier auf „Signalwörter", die die Verlaufsform einleiten, z. B. *at the moment, right now, today, this week*.

Übrigens: Die Form der einfachen Gegenwart und die *-ing*-Form können auch für zukünftige Ereignisse verwendet werden (siehe Sätze 4, 5 und 9).

34

Die Antworten, die **nicht** möglich sind:

1. **c)** Diese Antwort würde zu der Frage *What is a cinema like?* passen.
2. **b)** *Bye* wird am häufigsten verwendet. *Be seeing you* ist sehr locker und *Until next time* würde man sagen, wenn man sich regelmäßig zu etwas trifft, z. B. zum Sport.
3. **b)** Die Antwort wäre richtig, wenn es hieße: *No, I'm single.*
4. **b)** Dies ist eine allgemeine Aussage darüber, was man gerne trinkt, und keine Antwort auf die Frage, was man jetzt gerne trinken möchte. Ein *soft drink* ist ein alkoholfreies Getränk.
5. **d)** Diese Antwort passt zur Frage *Can you help me?*
6. **c)** Nur möglich im Spaß zwischen guten Freunden oder wenn jemand den Preis nicht nennen will.
7. **a)** Diese Antwort würde man auf die Frage *Would you like to play tennis (today/tomorrow)?* geben.
8. **b)**
9. **b)** *Stand up* bedeutet zwar aus dem Sitzen oder Liegen *aufstehen*, jedoch nicht morgens aus dem Bett aufstehen.
10. **a)** *I mean* bedeutet hier so viel wie *Was ich sagen will, ist … ,* z. B. auf die Frage *What do you mean?*

Tipp

Zeitangaben wie *zehn vor halb sieben* kann man nicht direkt ins Englische übersetzen. Richtig wären z. B. *just before half past seven* oder *twenty past six*. Obwohl *after* auch zeitlich verwendet werden kann, heißt es bei Uhrzeiten in britischem Englisch generell *past (nach)*.

35

1. **Falsch**. Mr Hege lebt in Deutschland.
2. **Falsch**. Er hatte Probleme mit Kaninchen und Hasen.
3. **Richtig**.
4. **Falsch**. Mr Hege probierte eine altmodische Methode aus.
5. **Falsch**. Er bat die Nachbarn um etwas Haar.
6. **Falsch**. Er züchtet spezielle Lupinen als Tierfutter.
7. **Richtig**.
8. **Falsch**. Mr Hege glaubt, dass die Kaninchen und Hasen den Geruch nicht mögen.
9. **Falsch**. Die Haare schaden den Kaninchen nicht.
10. **Falsch**. Nun ärgern sich die Kaninchen.

Tipp

Ist Ihnen aufgefallen, was die Wörter *hair* (Haar) und *hare* (Hase) gemeinsam haben? Richtig: Sie werden beide gleich ausgesprochen, und zwar auch im Plural: *hairs – hares*. Achtung: *Hair* wird normalerweise nur im Singular benutzt, z. B.: *He has dark hair. Hairs* – die Pluralform – wird nur dann verwendet, wenn ausdrücklich von einzelnen Haaren die Rede ist, z. B.: *He only had about two hairs left on his whole head.*

➔ Siehe hierzu auch Übung 17.

36

1. **had**; Signalwort: *last week*.
2. **found**
3. **were driving**, weil hier eine Unterbrechung des Fahrens erfolgt: *The motor stopped*.
4. **pushed**
5. **was rolling**, weil hier eine Unterbrechung des Hinabrollens erfolgt.
6. **telephoned**
7. **drove**
8. **were getting**
9. **hired**
10. **were riding**

Tipp

In einer Erzählung in der Vergangenheit werden die nacheinander ablaufenden Ereignisse in der einfachen Vergangenheit *(simple past)* beschrieben.
Die Verlaufsform in der Vergangenheit *(past progressive)* beschreibt Vorgänge/Handlungen, die von einem neu eintretenden Ereignis unterbrochen bzw. beendet werden, z. B. *As the car was rolling down the hill the door hit the tree.* Der gerade ablaufende Vorgang *(the car was rolling)* wurde durch ein neu eintretendes Ereignis *(hit the tree)* unterbrochen.

37

1. At **7.25** a.m.
2. **Four**. Die Züge um 7.25, 8.50, 10.10 und 10.50 Uhr.
3. The train that leaves at **17.45**.
4. At **16.57**.
5. **No**. Siehe Symbol *FX – Fridays excepted*.
6. **Four**. Die Züge um 14.30, 14.35, 18.40 und 19.00 Uhr mit dem Symbol *FO Fridays Only*.
7. **Reserve a seat**. Siehe Symbol R *(reservation compulsory – notwendig)*.
8. **One**. Nur der Zug mit Abfahrt um 16.05 Uhr von Paddington fährt durch. Bei allen anderen muss man in Exeter oder Newton Abbot umsteigen. Zu erkennen ist dies an der Art des Drucks (fett).
9. The train leaving at **14.35**. Alle anderen haben ein Restaurantsymbol.

Tipp

In London gibt es mehrere Hauptbahnhöfe, z. B. Euston (Richtung Nordwesten, z. B. Birmingham), King's Cross (Richtung Nordosten, z. B. Norfolk), Paddington (Richtung Südwesten, z. B. Bristol), Victoria (Richtung Süden, z. B. Brighton).

Exeter und Plymouth sind die größten Städte in Devon (auch Devonshire), und Penzance in Cornwall ist die weiteste Distanz von London mit einem durchgehenden Zug. Die Küste bei den Städten Torquay, Paignton und Brixham wird auch die „englische Riviera“ *(English Riviera)* genannt.

38

1. **horn, trumpet, clarinet**
2. **guitar, violin**
3. **song**
4. **drum**
5. **notes**
6. **singer**
7. **record**

C	X	T	C	S	O	N	G	X
L	G	R	H	I	P	D	A	S
A	G	U	I	T	A	R	V	L
R	Q	M	V	O	K	U	N	Z
I	S	P	H	I	L	M	O	H
N	R	E	C	O	R	D	T	O
E	Y	T	S	I	N	G	E	R
T	V	I	O	L	I	N	S	N

Tipp

Obwohl viele Musikinstrumente im Englischen und Deutschen ganz ähnlich heißen, werden sie unterschiedlich geschrieben. Auch hier ist Vorsicht vor den „falschen Freunden" geboten: Das erste Instrument für die meisten Kinder ist die *Blockflöte,* die im Englischen *recorder* heißt. Das Wort *flute* heißt *Querflöte.*

39

1. Would you mind opening the door?
2. How long have you lived here?
3. Where did you buy your new car?
4. Do you have a double room for one night?
5. Could you give me some information about this town please? Oder: *Please could you give me some information about this town?* Oder: *Could you please give me some information about this town?*
6. Would you recommend this restaurant to your friends?
7. How long have you worked here?
8. When did you fly to America?
9. How long have you been playing tennis?
10. When did you meet your wife for the first time?
11. How many times have you been to Malta?
12. Did you go to the cinema last night?
13. Have you read the new book by Grisham yet?

Tipp

Fast alle Verben erfordern eine Umschreibung mit dem Hilfsverb *do,* sofern eine Frage in der einfachen Gegenwart (siehe Frage 4) oder in der einfachen Vergangenheit (siehe Fragen 3, 8, 10 und 12) steht. Ausnahmen: *be, will/would, can/could, should, must, need.* Auch das Vollverb *do* muss in einer Frage mit *do* umschrieben werden, z. B.: *When do you do the housework?*

40

1. **ambulance**
2. **stretcher**
3. **hospital**
4. **injection**
5. **nurse**
6. **blood**
7. **tablet**
8. **doctor**
9. **operate**
10. **plaster**
11. **bandage**
12. **medicine**

Tipp

Falls Sie sich mit diesem Fachwortschatz nicht so gut auskennen, hier einige Worterklärungen:

ambulance	Krankenwagen
stretcher	Trage
hospital	Krankenhaus
injection	Spritze
nurse	Krankenschwester
male nurse	Krankenpfleger
blood	Blut
tablet	Pille, Tablette
doctor	Arzt; Ärztin
operate	operieren
plaster	*hier:* Gips (auch Heftpflaster)
bandage	Bandage, Verband
medicine	Medizin

Übrigens: Die Oberkrankenschwester im Krankenhaus in Großbritannien wird auch als *sister* bezeichnet. Der/die normale *Hausarzt/ärztin* ist der *GP (General Practitioner)*. Die *Praxis* ist die *surgery* oder *practice*. Nur bei speziellen Beschwerden wird man zum *Facharzt (specialist)* überwiesen.

In Großbritannien ist jeder – unabhängig von Alter, Beschäftigung, Staatsangehörigkeit usw. – automatisch über den staatlichen *National Health Service (NHS)* krankenversichert. Es gibt jedoch auch in England die Tendenz zur privaten Krankenversicherung, von der man sich eine bessere Versorgung verspricht.

41

A

1. Peru
2. Egypt
3. Rumania
4. Taiwan
5. Hungary

6. Austria
7. USA
8. Sweden
9. Thailand
10. Rwanda
11. Albania
12. Lebanon
13. Italy
14. Argentina

Lösung: **PERTH, AUSTRALIA**

B

1. ChiNa
2. Europe
3. SWeden

4. SwitZerland
5. MExico
6. BrAzil
7. SLovenia
8. BulgAria
9. HuNgary
10. InDia

Lösung: **NEW ZEALAND**

42

1. **big**, **large**; *great* heißt *großartig* und wird nicht bei der Angabe von Größen verwendet.
2. **front**
3. **full**
4. **sad**, **unhappy**
5. **hard**, **difficult**
6. **cold**, **cool**; *hot* kann sich auch auf eine scharf gewürzte Speise beziehen.
7. **light**, **bright**, **airy**
8. **closed**, **shut**
9. **slow**
10. **low**
11. **beautiful** oder **pretty** bei Frauen, **handsome** bei Männern. Für beide Geschlechter kann man **goodlooking** oder **attractive** sagen.
12. **bad**, **evil**
13. **new**, **modern**
14. **dry**
15. **dirty**
16. **light**
17. **short**
18. **weak**
19. **thin**
20. **blunt**

Tipp

Wenn man zum Ausdruck bringen will, dass jemand „nicht ganz helle“ ist, kann man das Wort *thick* benutzen. Es hat nichts mit der Figur zu tun, sondern bezieht sich in der Umgangssprache auf die Intelligenz. Das Gegenteil könnte z. B. *sharp* oder *smart* sein.

FERRY BOARDING CARD

Name: *Harry Hallen*

Address: *Königinstr. 7, Munich, Germany*

Postcode: *80539*

Your Age: 18-30 31–40 (41-50) 50+

1. How are you travelling:

   Foot (Car) Coach Freight

2. If travelling by car, what is the make of your car?

   Make (eg Ford) *BMW* Model (eg Sierra) *318 i*

   Registration No *M-HH 318*

3. What is your final destination? *Scotland (Highlands)*

4. What is the purpose of your journey?

   Touring Camping/caravan Skiing

   (Resort/City stay) Weekend break Day trip

5. When did you book your crossing? Month *April* 20 *04*

6. Are you Single (Married)

7. Do you have any children? (yes) no

8. What is your occupation? *car salesman*

44

1. BALLOON
2. KITE

3. TICKET
4. HOTEL
5. ENGINE

6. PLANE
7. GLIDER
8. RUNWAY
9. PASSENGER
10. PILOT
11. TRIP
2. FLIGHT ATTENDANT

Lösung: **AT THE AIRPORT**

Tipp

Hier noch einige Wörter, die Sie bei einer Flugreise vielleicht hören werden:
Jeder Flughafen hat einen *Empfangsbereich (arrivals)* und eine *Abflughalle (departures)*. Am *Abfertigungsschalter (check-in desk) checken Sie ein (check in)*. Sie bekommen eine *Bordkarte (boarding card)* und hören irgendwann den *Aufruf (call)*, dass Ihr *Flug (flight)* nun zum *Einsteigen (boarding)* bereit ist.

Jeweils vor dem *Start (take off)* und vor der *Landung (landing)* werden Sie aufgefordert, *sich anzuschnallen (fasten your seatbelt)*. Auf manchen Flügen haben Sie die Möglichkeit, *zollfrei einzukaufen (duty-free shopping)*.

45

1. **stealing**
2. **going**
3. **to go**
4. **staying**
5. **shutting**
6. **to go**
7. **to look**
8. **to work**
9. **visiting**
10. **calling**
11. **to eat**
12. **to travel**
13. **smoking**, weil sie wahrscheinlich ganz mit dem Rauchen aufgehört hat.
14. **Beide Formen sind richtig**.
15. **to smoke;** nach dem vierten Brief machte er eine Pause, um seine Pfeife zu rauchen.

Tipp

Nach manchen Verben können beide Formen verwendet werden – je nachdem, was man ausdrücken möchte. So z. B. nach *stop* (siehe Sätze 13 und 15), und nach den Verben *like, love, hate, begin, continue, go on, intend, prefer, start* und *try*.
I love/like swimming kann z. B. bedeuten, dass ich oft zum Schwimmen gehe, während *I love/like to swim* eher bedeutet, dass ich es gerne öfter täte, jedoch nicht dazu komme.

I remember talking to you about that. (Präsens) – *Ich erinnere mich (daran), mit dir darüber gesprochen zu haben.*
Aber: *I remembered to talk to you about that.* (Ich hätte es fast vergessen, dann habe ich aber doch noch daran gedacht.)

Übrigens: Bei Frage 5 antworten Sie mit *Yes*, wenn Sie das Fenster lieber offen hätten, und *No*, wenn Sie es schließen wollen.

➜ siehe auch Übung 4.

46

A

leopard – *Leopard*
duck – *Ente*
kiwi – *Kiwi*
ibis – *Ibis*
shark – *Hai*
kangaroo – *Känguru*
octopus – *Tintenfisch*
snake – *Schlange*
eagle – *Adler*
elephant – *Elefant*
tiger – *Tiger*
rhinoceros – *Nashorn*
spider – *Spinne*
rat – *Ratte*
turtle – *Wasserschildkröte*
elk – *Elch*
koala – *Koala*
alligator – *Alligator*
reindeer – *Rentier*
rabbit – *Kaninchen*

B

1. h)	**3. j)**	**5. g)**	**7. e)**	**9. c)**
2. f)	**4. i)**	**6. d)**	**8. b)**	**10. a)**

Tipp

Wissen Sie auch, wo die Tiere wohnen?

lion, fox, tiger:	den
fox:	lair
ibis, kiwi:	nest
eagle:	eerie
chicken:	coop
rabbits, rats:	burrow

bees:	hive
wild rabbit, hare:	warren
domestic rabbit:	hutch

Das deutsche Wort *Haustier* heißt im Englischen *pet*. *Nutztiere,* z. B. auf einem Bauerhof, sind im Englischen *domestic animals*.

47

1. **a)**; die Zeit bei b) ist falsch, da sie nur die Gegenwart beschreibt; c) *since* ist falsch.
2. **a)**; b) *since* ist falsch; c) die Zeit ist falsch.
3. **a)** Die Zeitangabe *yesterday* lässt nur die einfache Vergangenheit *(past simple)* zu.
4. **a)** Die Zeitangabe *when I was young* erfordert die einfache Vergangenheit.
5. **c)** Zeitangabe: *twenty years ago*.
6. **a)** Die Zeitangabe *since* erfordert *present perfect;* c) *my* ist falsch, *personal – persönlich*.
7. **b)** Die Zeitangabe *for* erfordert *present perfect.*
8. **a)** Zeitangabe: *last week*.
9. **a)** *for* erfordert *present perfect.*

Tipp

Und hier noch einmal zur Erinnerung:
In der einfachen Vergangenheit werden Handlungen/Ereignisse beschrieben, die in der Vergangenheit abgeschlossen wurden. „Signalwörter" sind z. B. *yesterday/when I was young/twenty years ago/last week*.

Das *Present Perfect* wird gebraucht, wenn der Zeitraum bzw. die Handlungen/Ereignisse nicht abgeschlossen sind bzw. wenn die Zeit keine Rolle spielt. „Signalwörter": *for, since*. Es ist sozusagen eine Brücke zwischen der Vergangenheit und der Gegenwart.

48

1. **Falsch**. Die Familie wollte zum Pferderennen.
2. **Richtig**
3. **Richtig**
4. **Richtig**
5. **Richtig**
6. **Falsch**. Eine Frau rief an.
7. **Falsch**. Das Auto wurde ungefähr eine halbe Stunde später angehalten.
8. **Richtig**
9. **Richtig**
10. **Richtig**

Tipp

In Newton Abbot werden überwiegend Pferderennen veranstaltet. Pferderennen und vor allem das damit verbundene Wetten sind in Großbritannien sehr beliebt. In jeder Stadt gibt es ein oder mehrere *Wettbüros (betting shops)*, auch *Turf (Pferderennbahn) accountants* genannt. In den Wettbüros kann man die einzelnen Rennen auf Bildschirmen verfolgen.

Die größten Pferderennen in Großbritannien sind das Derby (ohne Hindernisse) und der Grand National (mit hohen Hindernissen). In manchen Firmen werden für diese Rennen eigene Lotterien veranstaltet.

49

10 – 13 – 2 – 6 – 16 – 11 – 3 – 1 – 8 – 12 – 15 – 4 – 14 – 7 – 5 – 9 oder 8 – 15 – 2 – 10 – 16 – 9 – 3 – 1 – 6 – 14 – 13 – 4 – 12 – 11 – 5 – 7

Tipp

Im Allgemeinen können Sie zwischen drei Arten von Zimmern wählen: einem *Einzelzimmer (single room)*, einem *Doppelzimmer (double room)* mit einem großen *Doppelbett (double bed)* oder einem Doppelzimmer mit *zwei einzelnen Betten (twin beds)*.

Erkundigen Sie sich vorsichtshalber vorher, ob das Frühstück im Preis inbegriffen ist; in teuren Hotels wird es häufig extra berechnet. Sie können in der Regel zwischen einem eher kleinen Frühstück *(continental breakfast)* oder einem umfangreichen englischen Frühstück *(English breakfast)* wählen. Während Sie beim *continental breakfast* Toast, Aufschnitt, Käse, Marmelade und Müsli oder Cornflakes bekommen, umfasst das traditionelle englische Frühstück auch Dinge wie Bratwürstchen, gebratenen Speck mit Ei und vieles mehr.

50

1. **sheep**
2. **fish/fishes**. *We caught some fish.* Aber: *We caught five fish(es).*
3. **children**
4. **hair/hairs**. *The dog loses a lot of hair in the spring.* Aber: *She found two hairs in her soup.*
5. **deer**
6. **toys**
7. **women**
8. **dogs**
9. **data**
10. **cacti** oder **cactuses**
11. **advice**. *Some advice* oder *a piece of advice.*
12. **books**. Kann auch so viel wie *Bilanz/Konten* bedeuten.
13. **men**
14. **records**. Kann auch *Dokumente* oder *Schallplatten* bedeuten.
15. **news**. *A piece of news – eine Nachricht.*
16. **grass** (seltener: *grasses)*
17. **information**. *Some information, a piece of information.*
18. **beer/beers**. *I would like some beer.* Aber: *Three beers please!*
19. **people**. *Persons* wird eher im juristischen Zusammenhang verwendet (bei Gericht).
20. **coffee/coffees**. *Can I buy some coffee?* Aber: *Two coffees, please*. Der Plural kann hier, wie bei *grass* oder *beer*, auch verschiedene Sorten von etwas bedeuten.

Tipp

Manche Gegenstände gibt es im Englischen nur in der Pluralform, z. B. *jeans, scissors.* Will man hier von mehreren Hosen bzw. mehreren Scheren reden, nimmt man *a pair of* zur Hilfe, z. B. *two pairs of jeans, three pairs of scissors.*

Nicht zählbare Dinge wie Käse, Wein, Rasen o. ä. werden selten im Plural verwendet. In der Mehrzahl bezieht man sich meist auf verschiedene Sorten davon (siehe *grasses, beers, coffees*).

Übrigens: Der Plural *peoples* bezieht sich auf *people* in der Bedeutung *Volk/Völker.*

Glossar

Die folgenden Worterklärungen beziehen sich auf die Übungen in diesem Buch. Die Vokabeln haben zum Teil andere Bedeutungen.

1	
bunch of flowers	Blumenstrauß
heart shape	Herzform
landlord	(Kneipen-)Wirt
shelf	Regal
merry	fröhlich
bill	Rechnung
2	
bright	sonnig
4	
to borrow	borgen, sich leihen
5	
to be off	*hier:* schlecht, verdorben sein
upside down	verkehrt herum
clocking-in machine	Stechuhr
clay	Lehm
6	
leaf	Blatt
10	
wealth	Reichtum
rubbish	Abfall, Müll
sale	*hier:* Ausverkauf
11	
waist	Taille
12	
to manage to do sth.	es schaffen, etwas zu tun
spare time	Freizeit
fluent(ly)	fließend
drawer	Schublade
damage	Schaden
13	
tomboy	Wildfang
to vouch	sich verbürgen
horse chestnut tree	Rosskastanie
string	Schnur
savvy	schlau, geschickt

14

to slip on	anziehen
to hire	mieten, leihen

15

lie	Lüge
to be executed	hingerichtet werden
to parcel	verpacken
reindeer	Rentier
lung cancer	Lungenkrebs
famine	Hungersnot, Knappheit
Crimean War	Krimkrieg
Boer War	Burenkrieg
to abolish	abschaffen
message	*hier:* Spruch

16

accounts department	Buchhaltung (Abteilung)
impressive	beindruckend

17

slates	Schieferplatten
to look after	*hier:* pflegen
to fail	*hier:* nicht funktionieren
greedy	gefräßig
gipsy lady	Zigeunerin

18

Guy Fawkes Night	Jahrestag der Pulververschwörung
harvest	Ernte
settler	Siedler/in
patron saint	Schutzpatron/in

19

female	weiblich
majority	Mehrheit, Mehrzahl
sword	Schwert
stage show	Bühnenshow

22

slight illness	leichte Erkrankung
punishment	Strafe
speeding	Geschwindigkeitsüberschreitung
to sack	kündigen
event	Ereignis
written account	Bericht
unit	Einheit

23

main course	Hauptgang
to recommend	empfehlen

24

valid	gültig
delivery	Lieferung
to commence	beginnen

25

settee	Sofa
pillow	Kissen
to wipe	(ab-)wischen

26

to be dressed up	verkleidet sein
bride	Braut
thistle	Distel
vinegar	Essig
pudding	*hier:* Kuchen

27

pantyhose	Strumpfhose
billfold	Brieftasche
pumps/plimsoles	Turnschuhe
waistcoat	Weste

28

whitebait	Breitling
cod	Kabeljau

29

semi-detached house	Doppelhaushälfte
biro	Kugelschreiber
B & B (bed & breakfast)	Frühstückspension
lane	Sträßchen, Gasse, Spur
keyboard	Tastatur

30

servant	Diener
to be puzzled	verdutzt sein
appointment	Termin
fate	Schicksal

34

to be divorced	geschieden sein
soft drink	alkoholfreies Getränk
ugly	hässlich

35	
hopping mad	fuchsteufelswild
hare	Feldhase
lupin	Lupine
fence	Zaun
comb	Kamm
36	
holiday cottage	Ferienhäuschen
replacement	Ersatz
puncture	platter Reifen
37	
to provide	geben, zur Verfügung stellen
38	
brass	Messing
string instrument	Streichinstrument
40	
steep	steil
to bang	anschlagen
42	
towel	Handtuch
43	
number plate	Nummernschild
strangely	seltsamerweise
make of car	Automarke
destination	Reiseziel
purpose	Zweck
resort	Ferienort/-lager
occupation	Beruf
45	
thief	Dieb/in
to admit	zugeben, (zu)gestehen
48	
alert	Alarm
boot	*hier:* Kofferraum
to avoid	vermeiden
to spot	sichten
49	
suitable	passend
50	
deer	Hirsch, Reh